GAZETTEER OF THE
RAILWAYS OF WALES

Class 153 No 153382 is about to enter Sugar Loaf Tunnel with the 1105 Shrewsbury to Swansea service on 20 May 1995.

GAZETTEER OF THE
RAILWAYS OF WALES

A photographic record of the
British Rail network at privatisation

John Hillmer

·RAILWAY HERITAGE·
from
The NOSTALGIA *Collection*

The book is dedicated to the memory of
Bryan Wilson
who died in October 2007.
Bryan was a friend who was not only a highly respected
railway manager but also a dedicated railway historian known
for his passion for accuracy in all he did. Bryan loved Wales
and he and his wife Jill greatly enjoyed living in Deganwy.

First published in 2008

British Library Cataloguing in Publication Data

A catalogue record for this book is available from the
British Library.

ISBN 978 1 85794 303 0

Silver Link Publishing Ltd
The Trundle
Ringstead Road
Great Addington
Kettering
Northants NN14 4BW

Tel/Fax: 01536 330588
email: sales@nostalgiacollection.com
Website: www.nostalgiacollection.com

Printed and bound in the Czech Republic

All photographs are by the author unless otherwise
credited.

Bibliography and further reading

Baker, S. K. *Rail Atlas Great Britain & Ireland* (OPC/Ian Allan)

Barrie, D. S. M. *A Regional History of the Railways of Great Britain Volume 12: South Wales*
(2nd ed) (David & Charles, 1994)

Baughan, Peter E. *A Regional History of the Railways of Great Britain Volume 11: North and
Mid Wales* (2nd ed) (David & Charles, 1991)

British Rail Track Diagrams Parts 3 (Great Western) and 4 (London Midland) (Quail Map
Company)

British Railways Locomotives & Coaching Stock 1994 (Platform 5)

Deaves, Phil (collated by) *Signal Box prefix codes*
http://www.deaves47.users.btopenworld.com/signal/signal_boxes.htm

Kay, Peter and Coe, Derek *Signalling Atlas & Signal Box Directory* (2nd ed) (Signalling Record
Society)

Quick, M. E. *Railway Passenger Stations in England, Scotland and Wales: A chronology* (3rd ed)
(Railway & Canal Historical Society, 2005)

Rhodes, Michael and Shannon, Paul *Freight Only Volume 3 Wales & Scotland* (Silver Link
Publishing)

Shannon, Paul *Rail Freight since 1968: Coal* (Silver Link Publishing, 2006)

Wignall, C. J. *Complete British Railways Maps & Gazetteer from 1830-1981* (OPC, 1983)

Contents

Maps of the railways of Wales   6
Abbreviations   7

Introduction/Rhagarweiniad   11
Privatisation   13
Passenger services, mail/parcels trains and
  named trains, 1995   15
Freight services, 1995   20
  Freight flows in Wales, 1995   22
Loco depots, stabling and fuelling points, 1995   33
  Pool codes, winter 1995   40
  Summary of units and locomotives   40

British Rail stations in Wales, 1995   41
  Names of lines   42
  A-Z gazetteer of stations   43
  New stations and major alterations since
    privatisation   160

Signalling in Wales, 1995   165
A-Z of signal boxes open at the end of 1995   166

Of further interest

The Welsh Railways Research Circle brings together researchers and modellers who are interested not only in the main-line and branch railways of Wales and the Border Counties, but also the tramways, tramroads and the many rail-connected industrial locations across the Principality.

The main purpose of the Circle is to put members in touch with others of similar interest and to go some way to avoid duplication of research effort.

While many WRRC members research the pre-grouping aspects of railways in Wales, the group is keenly aware that even yesterday is now history. Potential new members with an interest in railways in Wales, including the privatised companies, are invited to contact the Circle's Membership Secretary; contact details are on the Circle's website: www.wrrc.org.uk.

The Signalling Record Society was founded in 1969 for the study of signalling operation and history in the British Isles and overseas. For membership details contact the Membership Secretary, Signalling Record Society, 38 Founceley Avenue, Dane End, Ware, Herts. SG12 ONQ. The website is www.s-r-s.org.uk. The Society is responsible for producing the *Signalling Atlas & Signal Box Directory* listed above.

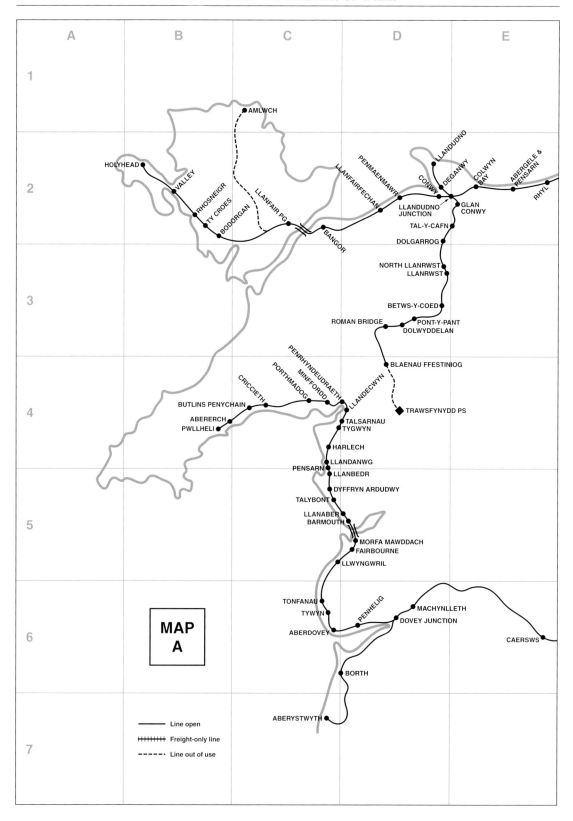

MAP
A

Line open
+++++++ Freight-only line
------ Line out of use

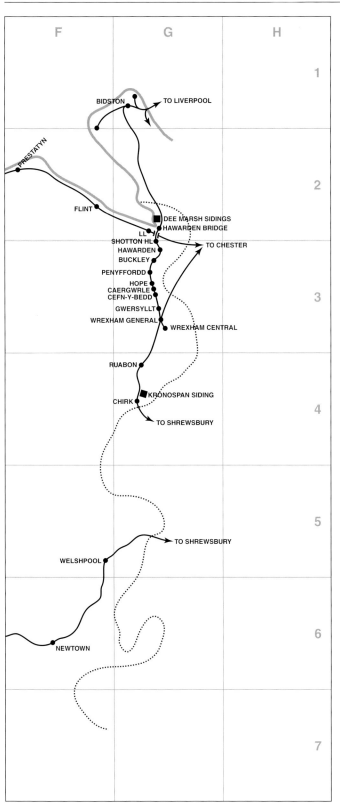

Abbreviations

A&WC	Aberystwyth & Welsh Coast Railway
ARC	Associated Road Stone
ASW	Allied Steel & Wire
BC	Borough Council
BR	British Rail/Railways
BS	British Steel
C&H	Chester & Holyhead Railway
Camb	Cambrian Railways
CC	County Council
DMU	Diesel multiple unit
DoT	Department of Transport
EEC	European Economic Community
EMU	Electric multiple unit
ERDF	European Regional Development Fund
EWS	English, Welsh & Scottish Railway
GCR	Great Central Railway
GWR	Great Western Railway
HST	High Speed Train
IC	InterCity
LMR	London Midland Region, British Railways
LMS	London Midland & Scottish Railway
LNER	London & North Eastern Railway
LNWR	London & North Western Railway
MGR	'Merry-go-round' (coal trains)
NSKT	No Signalman Key Token
PRNI	Project of Regional and National Importance
PS	Power station
Res	Rail Express Systems
RETB	Radio Electronic Token Block
RfD	Railfreight Distribution
RR	Regional Railways
RRy	Rhymney Railway
TOC	Train Operating Company
TOU	Train Operating Unit
TSG	Transport Supplementary Grant
TVR	Taff Vale Railway
V of G	Vale of Glamorgan
WR	Western Region, British Railways

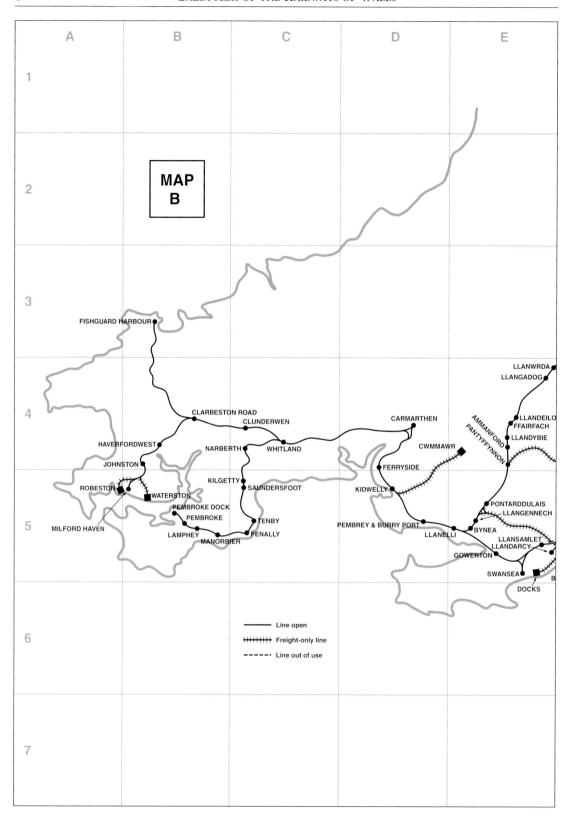

MAP
B

FISHGUARD HARBOUR

LLANWRDA
LLANGADOG

CLARBESTON ROAD
CLUNDERWEN
CARMARTHEN
LLANDEILO
FFAIRFACH
LLANDYBIE
HAVERFORDWEST
NARBERTH   WHITLAND
CWMMAWR
AMMANFORD
PANTYFFYNNON
JOHNSTON
FERRYSIDE
ROBESTON
WATERSTON
KILGETTY
SAUNDERSFOOT
KIDWELLY
PONTARDDULAIS
LLANGENNECH
PEMBROKE DOCK
MILFORD HAVEN
PEMBROKE
TENBY
PEMBREY & BURRY PORT
BYNEA
LAMPHEY   PENALLY
LLANELLI
LLANSAMLET
MANORBIER
LLANDARCY
GOWERTON
SWANSEA
DOCKS

Line open
Freight-only line
Line out of use

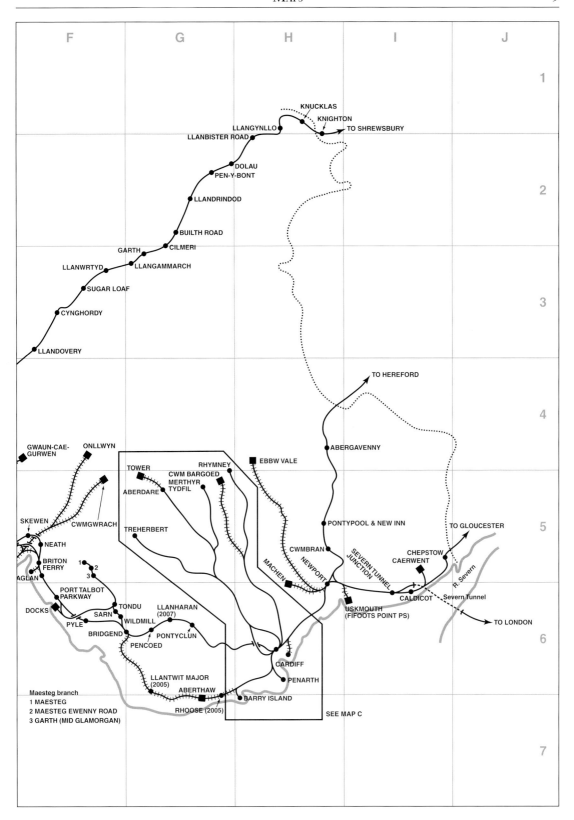

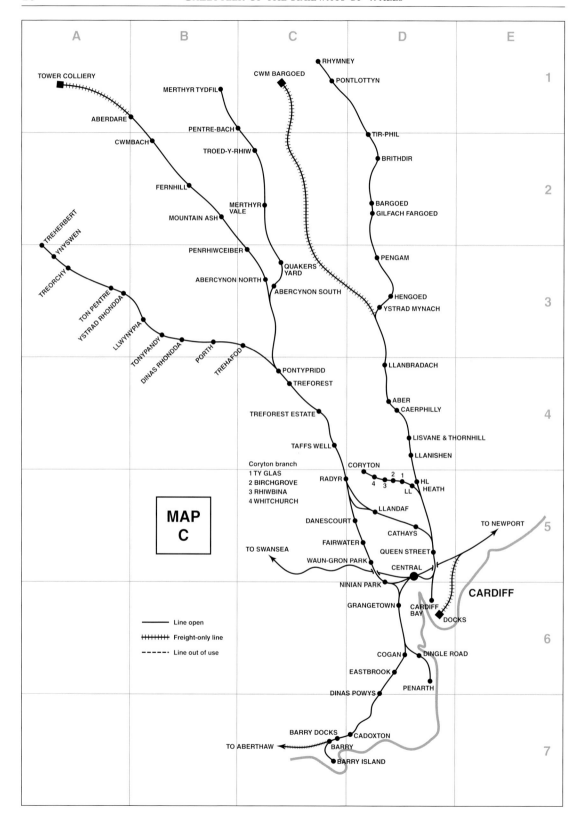

RHYMNEY

CWM BARGOED

TOWER COLLIERY

PONTLOTTYN

MERTHYR TYDFIL

ABERDARE

PENTRE-BACH

TIR-PHIL

CWMBACH

TROED-Y-RHIW

BRITHDIR

FERNHILL

MERTHYR VALE

BARGOED
GILFACH FARGOED

MOUNTAIN ASH

TREHERBERT
YNYSWEN

PENRHIWCEIBER

PENGAM

TREORCHY

QUAKERS YARD

ABERCYNON NORTH

TON PENTRE
YSTRAD RHONDDA

ABERCYNON SOUTH

HENGOED
YSTRAD MYNACH

LLWYNYPIA

TONYPANDY

DINAS RHONDDA

PORTH

TREHAFOD

LLANBRADACH

PONTYPRIDD

TREFOREST

ABER
CAERPHILLY

TREFOREST ESTATE

LISVANE & THORNHILL

TAFFS WELL

LLANISHEN

Coryton branch
1 TY GLAS
2 BIRCHGROVE
3 RHIWBINA
4 WHITCHURCH

CORYTON

RADYR

2 1

4 3

HL
HEATH

LL

MAP
C

LLANDAF

DANESCOURT

CATHAYS

TO SWANSEA

FAIRWATER

QUEEN STREET

TO NEWPORT

WAUN-GRON PARK

CENTRAL

NINIAN PARK

CARDIFF

GRANGETOWN

CARDIFF
BAY

DOCKS

——— Line open

COGAN

DINGLE ROAD

┼┼┼┼┼┼ Freight-only line

EASTBROOK

- - - - - Line out of use

PENARTH

DINAS POWYS

BARRY DOCKS

CADOXTON

TO ABERTHAW

BARRY

BARRY ISLAND

Introduction

At the 1923 grouping most of the individual railway companies were amalgamated into the 'Big Four' – the Great Western Railway, the London, Midland & Scottish Railway, the London & North Eastern Railway and the Southern Railway – marking the end of an era that had commenced when the first railways were built in the United Kingdom. This situation lasted until 1948 when nationalisation took place and the four companies were brought together as British Railways, marking the end of the second era. So things remained until 1993 when the Railways Act, authorising the privatisation of BR, became law, although the process did not begin in earnest until 1995, ultimately bringing the third (nationalised) era to a close in 1997.

The object of this book is to present a photographic record of all the British Rail stations open in Wales at the end of 1995, being the last year that BR remained a fully nationalised and integrated system. In addition, it summarises the passenger and freight services and details the freight flows in 1995, lists locomotive depots, stabling and re-fuelling points, and illustrates all the signal boxes open at the end of 1995, together with additional photographs to illustrate the types of locomotive and units in use. With privatisation completed, it seemed that the then recently elected Labour Government (in May 1997) was unlikely to reverse the procedure, although it had said that it would impose a stricter regulation of Railtrack (which controlled rail access) and did not rule out the possibility of re-acquiring shares in Railtrack as resources allowed.

Unless otherwise stated the photographs were taken by myself mainly during the years 1993-95. I would like to place on record my thanks to all the people who have so freely given of their time and expertise, in particular Dai Bryan, Gwyn Briwnant-Jones, Ray Caston, John P. McCrickard, Tony Miller, Brian Mills, Rowland Pittard, Paul Shannon, Dave Walters and the late Bryan Wilson. Their help has been immeasurable. In addition I would also like to acknowledge the information supplied by different sections of Arriva Trains Wales, Railtrack, Central Trains Ltd, and South Glamorgan County Council. The responsibility for any errors or omissions is entirely mine. My grateful thanks also go to Gwyn Taylor-Williams for the translation of this Introduction.

John Hillmer
September 2007

Rhagarweiniad

Yn y Grwpio 1923 fe gyfunwyd y rhan helaethaf o'r cwmniau rheilffyrdd unigol i bedwar gr?p – y 'Big Four' – y 'Great Western Railway', y 'London, Midland & Scottish Railway', y 'London & North Eastern Railway' a'r 'Southern Railway', yn dirwyn i ben gyfnod oedd wedi cychwyn pan adeiladwyd y rheilffyrdd cyntaf ym Mhrydain Fawr. Fe barhaodd y sefyllfa yma hyd 1948 pan fu gwladoliad o'r diwydiant a chyfunwyd y pedwar i'r Rheilffyrdd Prydeinig, yn dynodi diwedd yr ail gyfnod. Felly yr arhosodd pethau, hyd 1993 pan ddaeth y Deddf Rheilffyrdd oedd yn awdurdodi preifateiddio BR yn gyfraith, er na gychwynodd y broses o ddifrif tan 1995, yn y pen draw yn dod â'r trydydd gyfnod (gwladoledig) i ben yn 1997.

Bwriad y llyfr hwn yw cyflwyno cofnod ffotograffig o bob gorsaf Rheilffyrdd Prydeinig (Railtrack) oedd ar agor ar ddiwedd 1995, sef y flwyddyn ddiwethaf i Rheilffyrdd Prydeinig fod yn gyfundrefn gwbl wladolig ac integredig. Yn ogystal, er mwyn crynhoi'r gwasanaethau teithwyr a chludiant nwyddau, manylu ar y llif cludiant nwyddau yn 1995, yn ogystal â 'locomotive depots', mannau cadw 'locomotives' ac ail lenwi tanwydd, lluniau o bob blwch signal oedd ar agor ar ddiwedd 1995, gyda lluniau ychwanegol i ddangos y math o 'locomotive' ac unedau ddefnyddiwyd. Gyda phreifateiddio wedi ei gwblhau 'roedd yn debyg na fyddai'r Llywodraeth Lafur, oedd newydd ddod i rym, yn gwrthdroi'r drefn, er eu bod wedi dweud y byddent yn rheoli 'Railtrack' (oedd yn rheoli mynediad i'r cledrau) yn fwy llym, ac nad oeddynt wedi diystyru y posibilrwydd o ail-gaffael cyfrandaliadau yn 'Railtrack' fel y byddai adnoddau yn caniatau.

Oni nodir yn wahanol tynnwyd y lluniau gennyf i yn ystod y tair blynedd o 1993-95 yn bennaf. Hoffwn gofnodi fy niolch i bawb sydd wedi rhoi yn hael o'u hamser a'u harbenigedd, yn enwedig Dai Bryan, Gwyn Briwnant-Jones, Ray Caston, John P. McCrickard, Tony Miller, Brian Mills, Rowland Pittard, Paul Shannon, Dave Walters a'r diweddar Bryan Wilson. Mae eu cymorth wedi bod yn amhrisiadwy. Hefyd, hoffwn gydnabod gyda diolch yr wybodaeth a dderbyniwyd gan 'Railtrack', 'Central Trains Ltd', Trenau Arriva Cymru a Chyngor Sir De Morgannwg. 'Rwy'n cymryd cyfrifoldeb personol am unrhyw wallau. 'Rwyf yn ddiolchgar hefyd i Gwyn Taylor-Williams am gyfieithu'r rhagarweiniad yma.

John Hillmer
Medi 2007

With the familiar outline of Conwy Castle as a backdrop, Class 31 Nos 31229+31512 cross the Conwy estuary, between Conwy and Llandudno Junction, with a loaded ballast train from Penmaenmawr to Warrington Arpley on 6 December 1996.

Privatisation

As rail privatisation approached, many changes had already taken place. Sectorisation into separate units such as Intercity, Regional Railways, Freight, etc, was followed by the formation of independent companies renting track usage from Railtrack. At the end of 1995 the Train Operating Units (TOUs) running trains in South Wales were Cardiff Railways Co Ltd, Great Western Trains Co Ltd, and South Wales & West Railways Ltd, the latter two with headquarters in Swindon.

Further north, the 'Heart of Wales' (Central Wales) line was operated by South Wales & West Railways, but the routes from Shrewsbury to Aberystwyth and Pwllheli, and Wolverhampton to Chester, were the responsibility of Central Trains Ltd, with headquarters in Birmingham. Services on the North Wales coast line were mainly operated by North West Regional Railways Ltd (HQ in Manchester) with InterCity West Coast Ltd running the Euston to Holyhead trains.

Freight services in Wales were primarily operated by Transrail (HQ in Crewe), being one of the three UK freight operating companies (the other two being Mainline Freight and Loadhaul). Automotive and 'Connectrail' services were run by Railfreight Distribution (RfD) with HQ at Paddington. In addition, Freightliner 1995 was responsible for all Freightliner services. Finally, Rail Express Systems (Res) operated the mail and parcels trains, as well as the Royal Train. Each company operated its own fleet of locomotives and rolling-stock.

However, on 9 December 1995 Res was sold to a US consortium led by Wisconsin Central at a cost of £27.5 million. The sale included 164 locomotives (27 Class 08 shunters, 117 Class 47s, 15 Class 86s and 5 Class 90s) together with Class 307 EMU driving trailers (for conversion to Propelling Control Vehicles), vans and barrier wagons.

Before the end of 1995 the Government awarded the first tranche of franchises. The large bus operator Stagecoach was successful in its bid to operate trains out of Waterloo (with some direct services to South Wales), but, with much greater importance for Wales, Great Western Holdings was awarded the franchise (7 to 10 years) for services from Paddington to South Wales. The consortium included FirstBus, another major bus operator.

Further franchises were allocated during the years 1996 and 1997, with Railtrack itself being floated on the Stock Market in May 1996.

As far as freight was concerned, on 24 February 1996 the Government announced that the successful bidder for the three freight-operating companies (Transrail, Mainline Freight and Loadhaul) was North & South Railways (the UK subsidiary of Wisconsin Central Transportation Corporation), which had paid a reported £225 million, thus adding to its previous purchase of Rail Express Systems (Res). The initial operating name adopted was 'English, Welsh & Scottish Railway Ltd', later reduced to the initials EWS on locomotives, etc. For fuller details on this subject, Ian Allan published a book in 1996 by John Glover called *National Railways – a Guide to the Privatised Railway*.

North Wales variety: Class 156 No 156441 is seen on 22 June 1993 near Llanfair PG with the 1500 Holyhead to Llandudno service. In the background can be seen the Marquis of Anglesey's column, from the top of which there are wonderful views across the Menai Strait and beyond to Snowdonia.

The second photograph shows Class 37 No 37407 *Loch Long* in Regional Railways livery at Bangor with the 1330 Holyhead to Manchester Victoria train on 25 March 1994.

Finally an unidentified Class 43 HST passes through Bagillt with the 1430 Holyhead to Euston service on 29 June 1997. The Dee estuary lies over to the right.

Passenger services, mail/parcels trains and named trains, 1995

North Wales services consisted of three trains daily in each direction between London Euston and Holyhead (HST IC 125s or, on occasion, loco-hauled stock with a Class 47), frequent services from Birmingham, Crewe or Manchester terminating at Llandudno, Bangor or Holyhead, and loco-hauled stock (primarily using Class 37s but with 31s and 47s filling in as required) or DMUs – usually 'second generation', but with some services operated by 'Heritage' Class 101 units. Certain trains to and from Holyhead were timed to connect with the Irish ferries.

The branch line from Llandudno Junction to Blaenau Ffestiniog was operated by DMUs, with a Monday-Saturday service of six trains daily in each direction (with a Sundays-only service in mid-summer), the journey taking an hour from the Junction. Most trains started from and returned to Llandudno, the terminus of the only other passenger branch in North Wales. Services from Llandudno to Bangor/Holyhead had to reverse at Llandudno Junction station, then called at the intermediate stations, several of which were 'request stops', as were a number on the Conwy Valley line to Blaenau Ffestiniog.

There was a direct service between North and South Wales, an early-morning departure from Holyhead arriving in Cardiff some 5 hours later. The train, formed of a Class 158 two-car 'Express' DMU, did not take the most direct line via Wrexham (which would have involved a reversal at Chester) but ran via Crewe and Shrewsbury. It returned from Cardiff in the early evening.

Between Chester and Flint the main line passes under the Bidston to Wrexham Central line at Shotton, where there is an interchange station with 'High Level' and 'Low Level' platforms. Services to Wrexham were DMU-operated, including single-car Class 153s, offering an hourly service. A reduction of fares during 1995 was rewarded with a most encouraging increase in passenger numbers using the route. The line to Wrexham General and Shrewsbury leaves the North Wales coast line at Saltney Junction, just to the west of Chester, with DMU services (usually Class 158s or 153s) between Chester and Wolverhampton, although only a few miles of the line lie within Wales – between Rossett and Chirk.

West of Shrewsbury two important routes led into Wales. At Sutton Bridge Junction a single track leaves the Hereford line and crosses the border between Westbury and Welshpool, leading on to Newtown, Caersws, Machynlleth and Dovey Junction, where the line to Borth and Aberystwyth heads south and that to Pwllheli northwards, calling at numerous stations en route, including the important town of Barmouth. All services were operated by Class 153, 156 or 158 DMUs.

Returning to lines leaving Shrewsbury to the south, the other one that concerns us is to Hereford and beyond. At Craven Arms the Central Wales (or 'Heart of Wales') line leaves to the south-west, entering Wales at Knighton, then travels through delightful countryside, emerging on to the South Wales main line, just east of Llanelli, at Llandeilo Junction. There are 25 stations within Wales (including Knighton, where the station is actually just in England). Many are request stops, including Sugar Loaf Halt, which caters for hikers and is used mainly in the summer months. The line does, however,

Left Class 101 DMU No 101685, in green 'Heritage' livery, stands in the west-end bay at Llandudno Junction with the 1318 service to Holyhead on 15 November 1994.

Below Class 158 No 158757, near Llanddulas forming the 1322 Bangor to Crewe service, heads away towards Abergele & Pensarn on 22 July 1994.

Right Class 142 No 142058 pauses at Hawarden with a Bidston-Wrexham Central service on 4 June 1993.

HSTs operated the services to Paddington from Swansea and Cardiff. On 28 November 1995 power car No 43151, at the head of a Swansea-Paddington train, enters Cardiff Central station.

serve the larger towns of Llandrindod Wells, Llandovery and Llandeilo.

The service was sparse, with only four trains in each direction Mondays to Saturdays, and while in the summer there were Sunday services known as 'Heart of Wales Ramblers', there was no similar service in the winter timetable period. The line was operated by DMUs – usually single-car Class 153s. Services started or terminated at Swansea, having to reverse at Llanelli.

From Craven Arms the main route runs south to Hereford and beyond to Newport. After entering Wales a few miles north of Abergavenny, there are stations at Pontypool & New Inn and Cwmbran en route to Newport before the line joins the South Wales main line at Maindee West Junction, just east of Newport. Trains on this line basically ran from Cardiff to Manchester or Liverpool, although some services started from Milford Haven, Bridgend or Pembroke Dock. Two-car Class 158s dominated, with some Class 153s and occasional substitutes of loco-hauled stock, and one regular such timetabled train on Friday evenings from Cardiff to Manchester Oxford Road, and some Sunday trains between the Cardiff and Liverpool, were hauled by a Class 37 locomotive (which subsequently ceased). Regional Railways promoted services under their 'Alphaline' title, offering seat reservations,

air-conditioning, a trolley buffet service and telephones on the Class 158 DMUs.

The line from Gloucester enters Wales just to the east of Chepstow and joins the main line from Bristol at Severn Tunnel Junction. Trains were basically Nottingham/Birmingham New Street to Cardiff/West Wales, also operated by Class 158 units, but there was one Class 37-hauled service on Sunday evenings between Cardiff and Birmingham New Street and return. There was an approximate 2-hour service from Nottingham or Birmingham New Street calling at Chepstow and Caldicot, but Severn Tunnel Junction was served mostly by the DMUs on the Bristol to Cardiff services.

Within Wales, the South Wales main line runs from the Severn Tunnel through to Swansea and beyond to Carmarthen, Pembroke Dock (this line includes Tenby), Milford Haven and Fishguard Harbour. Normally all trains stopped at Newport, and those that continued beyond Cardiff usually served Bridgend, most calling at Port Talbot and Neath, and some at the intermediate stations serving the smaller communities, although Pontyclun and Pencoed are primarily served by Cardiff to Maesteg trains and Pyle, Briton Ferry, Skewen and Llansamlet services mainly by Cardiff/Bridgend to Swansea trains. There was an hourly service west of Swansea to Carmarthen, usually worked by Class 143s with occasional 153s and 158s. The

'Valleys' services: Class 143 No 143606 stands at the new Merthyr Tydfil station with a service to Penarth on 28 June 1996, and Class 150 No 150278 is seen at Treherbert with a service to Barry Island on 26 April 1995.

principal trains were those between Swansea/Cardiff and London Paddington, all operated by IC 125 HST Class 43s. Two services ran to and from Fishguard Harbour connecting with the ferries to Rosslare in Ireland. South Wales had three trains daily (Monday to Saturday), one from Carmarthen and two from Cardiff, to London Waterloo, where there were connections with Eurostar trains to Paris and Brussels via the Channel Tunnel. Swansea had a through train to York and another cross-country service operated between West Wales and Salisbury/ Portsmouth, the latter mostly using Class 158 'Sprinters', while from Cardiff there were direct trains to Weston-super-Mare, Paignton, Penzance, and weekend services from

Milford Haven through to Brighton and Cardiff to Weymouth.

Cardiff Central is the hub of the intensive 'Valleys' services. There are three terminal stations on the south side of Cardiff at Barry Island, Penarth and Cardiff Bay. Services from these stations run to the valleys north of Cardiff – Rhymney, Coryton, Aberdare, Merthyr Tydfil and Treherbert. The suburban stations on the Ninian Park line are served by trains from Central to Radyr ('City Line'). Valleys services were operated by DMU Classes 143 and 150, although from the autumn of 1995 certain peak-hour trains consisted of loco-hauled coaches, hired from Waterman Railways, between Cardiff and Rhymney. The

Class 47 No 47714 passes Pyle with 1A71, the Swansea to Paddington parcels, on 9 May 1995. The engine is in Res (Rail Express Systems) livery.

TPOs ran regularly between South Wales and Paddington, and this photograph of a Royal Mail NSA van was taken at Cardiff Central on 6 October 1994. These trains were also operated by Res. The last TPO ran in 2003 after Royal Mail decided to cease using rail by March 2004.

Maesteg branch leaves the main line just west of Bridgend station at Llynfi Junction.

Mail trains ran between Swansea and Paddington via Bristol Temple Meads, and from Plymouth to Crewe and Glasgow to Bristol via Shrewsbury on the 'Marches Line', the former calling at Cardiff and the latter at Newport, requiring the locomotives to 'run round' before resuming their journeys.

TPO and parcels trains were operated by Rail Express Systems (Res), with locomotives and vans in red livery. There were no mail/parcels trains on the North Wales coast line, but mention should be made of the Crewe test train, which ran 'as required' from Crewe to Holyhead, normally with two red-liveried Class 47 diesel locomotives and similarly painted parcels/mail vans, operated by Res, as a means of testing recently out-shopped locomotives from Crewe.

Named trains

In 1995 there were a number of named trains running in Wales:

The 'Irish Mail' between Euston and Holyhead
The 'Irish Mancunian' between Manchester Victoria and Holyhead
Y 'Ddraig Gymreig'/The 'Welsh Dragon' between Euston and Holyhead
The 'Emerald Isle Express' between Birmingham New Street and Holyhead
'St David Pullman' between Paddington and Swansea
The 'Hibernian' between Fishguard Harbour and Paddington
'Red Dragon Pullman' between Swansea and Paddington

All but the last-named had reverse workings.

Freight services, 1995

Despite the heavy loss of freight to road haulage over the years, the vast cut-back of the coalfields and effects of the recession during the 1990s, there remained considerable freight traffic within the Principality.

In North Wales there were up to three trains a day carrying stone from the quarry distribution point at Penmaenmawr to various destinations, mainly ballast for railway use. Nuclear waste was carried from Valley on Anglesey to Sellafield, coal from Point of Ayr Colliery in Clwyd to Fiddlers Ferry Power Station, chemicals from Hull (Saltend) to Mostyn Docks, and timber was brought from Scotland to Shotton Paper on Deeside. A very important flow was steel coil from Llanwern/Margam in South Wales to British Steel at Shotton, together with some return scrap metal from Shotton to Llanwern.

There were no freight services on the Cambrian lines to Pwllheli or Aberystwyth, nor on most of the length of the Central Wales line, but the Marches line ('North and West' route) from Newport to Hereford and beyond carried regular traffic consisting of Freightliners, the aforementioned steel coil trains and other flows, including china clay slurry from Burngullow to Irvine in Scotland, scrap metal

from Trafford Park to Cardiff and vinyl chloride monomer from Burn Naze to Barry.

The situation in South Wales was vastly different, with quite heavy and regular freight. Aberthaw Power Station received up to nine coal trains each weekday, and steel was dispatched to a number of destinations both within and beyond Wales. Imported coal and iron ore were moved from Port Talbot to Llanwern, and there were arrivals of scrap metal from various parts of the UK at Cardiff Tidal (Allied Steel & Wire). Petroleum products were sent out from the refineries at Milford Haven and there were Freightliner trains in and out of Cardiff Pengam connecting with Crewe and Coatbridge, near Glasgow. Other miscellaneous trains included the RfD 'Connectrail' and Transrail 'Enterprise' services; the former catered for European traffic via the Channel Tunnel and the latter for domestic wagonload traffic. Freight services have to be flexible to the needs and changes of their customers' businesses, resulting in continual gains and losses. Transrail was the main provider of freight services within Wales, with RfD (Railfreight Distribution) handling 'Connectrail', and automotive trains with Freightliner 1995 operating its own services.

Stabled at Newport on 3 August 1995 is Class 97/08 No 97806 with the Severn Tunnel Junction train, normally kept at Sudbrook. Note the Welsh Dragon below the number on the cab side. In the background can be seen the Newport Civic Centre.

Through traffic: On 6 January 1995 Class 56 No 56056 passes Wrexham General station with empty OTA timber wagons from Shotton Paper to Warrington Arpley.

In the second picture another Class 56, No 56044 *Cardiff Canton Quality Assured* passes through Newport with a westbound train of bogie tanks on 4 April 1996.

Finally, Class 47 No 47222, bearing Railfreight Distribution diamonds, heads west through Cardiff Central with empty MAT car-carrying wagons on 8 June 1995.

Finally there was a variety of trains serving the railway industry itself – loco fuel, permanent way, Severn Tunnel maintenance, civil engineers trains, breakdown trains, etc.

Looking into the future one could only hope that the railways would attract more freight, and undoubtedly the opening of the Channel Tunnel was expected to help in this direction. There were a number of private sidings out of use, such as those at the Kronospan Works at Chirk (subsequently back in use, bringing in timber as well as a few trial outward movements of chipboard) and at Aberystwyth (Shell). No doubt English Welsh & Scottish Railways will be keen to attract as much freight

traffic as possible back to rail. Although freight traffic ceased on the Amlwch branch (to Associated Octel) in 1994 and is unlikely to return, at least it is hoped that in the future the line may be run as a tourist attraction. (In 2007 the track remained in situ although the branch had been disconnected from the main line.)

Freight flows in Wales, 1995

Freight flows varied from regular, sometimes daily, workings to occasional and 'as required' services. The following is a guide to freight operations during 1995. (Return empties are not shown.)

Yard/siding(s)	Inwards from	Traffic	Outwards to	Traffic
ABERTHAW POWER STATION	Avonmouth	Coal		
	Cardiff Docks	Coal (ceased Oct 95)		
	Cardiff Docks, Minimet	Fuel oil		
	Cwmbargoed	Coal		
	Cwmgwrach	Coal		
	Steel Supply, Jersey Marine	Coal		
BAGLAN BAY	Hull (Saltend)	Acetic acid	Hull (Saltend)	Chemicals
	Humber Oil Refinery	Propylene LPG	Powell Dyffryn, Barry Docks	Styrene (ceased 1995)
			Stalybridge	Styrene
BARRY DOCKS (BP and Dow Chemicals)	Baglan Bay	Chemicals (via RfD)		
	Burn Bay	Vinyl chloride monomer		
	Hull (Saltend)	Chemicals		
BRIDGEND (Ford)	Halewood and Dagenham	Automotive components	Halewood, Dagenham and Europe	Completed engines

Class 09 No 09107 passes through Barry Docks station with a single bogie tank on a local trip working on 21 September 1994.

Class 37/7 No 37802 is seen at Barry with hooded coal hoppers on 21 September 1994. This was a Cardiff Canton-based engine carrying the Transrail coal sector diamonds.

Yard/siding(s)	Inwards from	Traffic	Outwards to	Traffic
CARDIFF (Canton Depot)	Fawley	Locomotive fuel oil		
CARDIFF DOCKS (Coastal Sidings)	Allied Steel & Wire	Rods and wire steel bars		
	Coed Bach	Containerised coal		
	Gwaun-Cae-Gurwen	Containerised coal		
	Onllwyn	Containerised coal		
CARDIFF DOCKS (Fletchers Wharf)			Aberthaw PS	Coal (Ryans) (ceased Oct 1995)
CARDIFF DOCKS (Minimet oil loading sidings)			Aberthaw PS	Fuel oil
			Didcot	Fuel oil
			Llanwern	Fuel oil
			St Helens (Pilkingtons)	Fuel oil
CARDIFF ISIS LINK	Mainland Europe	Steel	Mainland Europe	Steel
CARDIFF PENGAM (Freightliner Terminal)	Coatbridge (Glasgow)	Freightliner	Coatbridge (Glasgow)	Freightliner
	Crewe (Basford Hall)	Freightliner	Crewe (Basford Hall)	Freightliner
(Portions from/to Felixstowe, Tilbury, Liverpool Seaforth)				
	Lynemouth	Aluminium ingots	Southampton	Freightliner
	Southampton	Freightliner		
CARDIFF TIDAL (Allied Steel & Wire, Tremorfa and Rod Mill)	Ashburys (Manchester)	Scrap metal (ceased 1995)	Brierley Hill	Steel bars and reinforcing coils
	Braunstone Gate (Leicester)	Scrap metal (ceased Dec 1995)	Burton-on-Trent	Steel bars and reinforcing coils
	Dee Marsh	Scrap metal (occasional)	Cardiff Coastal Sidings	Steel bars and reinforcing coils
	Exeter	Scrap metal	Cardiff Docks	Steel bars and reinforcing coils
	Hamworthy	Imported cold reduced steel coil	Mainland Europe	Steel bars and reinforcing coils

Above This is Pengam Freightliner Terminal, on the down side of the South Wales main line between Newport and Cardiff. On 28 August 1998 No 37897, carrying the Transrail 'T' logo, passes the entrance to the terminal with 6V55, the Northwich to Cardiff Tidal oil empties. The Tidal Sidings are nearby and include Allied Steel & Wire Tremorfa Works. The Freightliner terminal was planned for closure in 1999 when it would be replaced by Wentloog, 2 miles to the east. *P. D. Shannon*

Below The entrance to the large Cardiff Tidal Yard was on the down side of the line. It was the collecting point for traffic to and from Allied Steel & Wire plants, and also handled flows to and from the docks. On 17 July 1997 No 08955 is seen shunting BDA wagons, photographed looking north. *P. D. Shannon*

Yard/siding(s)	Inwards from	Traffic	Outwards to	Traffic
CARDIFF TIDAL (cont)	Handsworth Kingsbury	Scrap metal	Mossend (Glasgow)	Steel bars and reinforcing coils
	Saltley	Scrap metal	Newport	Steel bars and reinforcing coils
	Scunthorpe and Aldwarke	Semi-finished steel	Southampton	Steel bars and reinforcing coils
	Swindon	Scrap metal	Swansea Docks	Steel bars and reinforcing coils
	Trafford Park	Scrap metal	Wakefield	Steel bars and reinforcing coils
	Willesden	Scrap metal	Warrington (Dallam)	Steel bars and reinforcing coils
COED BACH (Washery)	Cwmmawr	Coal	Cardiff Coastal Sidings	Containerised coal (Cawoods)
			Deepdale (Preston)	Household coal (ceased 1995)
			Gobowen via Margam and Bescot	Household coal/'Enterprise'
			Hull (Kingston coal terminal)	Cawoods container (one trial)
			Immingham	Anthracite duff (containerised)
			Mossend (Cadzow)	Anthracite
			Seaforth (Liverpool)	Cawoods coal (ceased 1995)
			Swansea Docks	Coal containers (for Eire)
			Swansea Docks (Burrows Sidings)	Anthracite duff
			West Drayton	Household coal
CWMBARGOED (Opencast)			Aberthaw PS	MGR coal
			Westbury via Barry	Coal
CWMGWRACH (Drift mine)			Aberthaw PS	Coal
CWMMAWR (Opencast)			Coed Bach Washery	Coal
DEE MARSH (Shotton)	Llanwern	Steel coil (for BS)	Llanwern	Scrap metal
	Margam	Steel coil (for BS)		
	Scotland (Elgin, Huntly, Inverness, Inverurie)	Timber (for Shotton Paper)		
EBBW VALE (Steelworks)	Margam	Steel coil	Westhoughton (Bolton)	Tin plate
			Wisbech	Tin plate
			Worcester	Tin plate
GWAUN-CAE-GURWEN (Opencast Disposal Point)			Cardiff Docks	Containerised coal (Cawoods)
			Seaforth (Liverpool)	Containerised coal (Cawoods) (ceased)
			West Drayton	Coal (very occasional)

Llandudno Junction Yard was opposite the station on the down side of the line. Looking east on 28 January 1994, Nos 31304+31275 have propelled into the yard a nuclear flask from Trawsfynydd, which will later be attached to those from Valley before going forward to Warrington and on to Sellafield. Both locos bear the black diamonds of Trainload Coal and were in pool code FCFN based at Toton, which also included Nuclear Flask Traffic. Beyond, No 37422 is stabled, and in the distance No 37503 is on a loaded ballast train.

Yard/siding(s)	Inwards from	Traffic	Outwards to	Traffic
HOLYHEAD (Anglesey Aluminium Metal Ltd)	Humber	Petroleum, coke		
HOLYHEAD (BR Depot)	Stanlow	Loco fuel oil		
LLANDARCY			Grain (Kent)	Bitumen
			Llanwern	Heated fuel oil
LLANDUDNO JUNCTION (Holding sidings, staging only)	Valley	Nuclear waste flasks	Arpley/Sellafield	Nuclear waste flasks
	Trawsfynydd	Nuclear waste flasks (ceased 1995)	Arpley/Sellafield	Nuclear waste flasks
LLANDUDNO JUNCTION (Glan Conwy Sidings)	Gascoigne Wood (Milford)	Household coal (trial movements)		
LLANWERN	Cardiff Docks	Oil	Ebbw Vale	Hot-rolled steel coil
	Daw Mill	Coal (temporary)	Mainland Europe	Hot-rolled steel coil
	Hem Heath (Trentham)	Coal (temporary)	Round Oak	Cold reduced steel coil
	Llandarcy	Heated fuel oil	Shotton (BS)	Hot-rolled steel coil
	Margam	Steel	Trostre	Hot-rolled steel coil
	Margam	Coal		
	Port Talbot	Iron ore		
	Shotton (BS)	Scrap metal		
	Silverdale Colliery	Coal (regular)		
MACHEN QUARRY			Newport (East Usk Yard)	Stone (ballast)
MARGAM (Knuckle Yard)	Eastleigh/ Bournemouth	Units for scrap at Gwent Demolition	Cardiff Tidal/ Newport/ Warrington	Enterprise
	Fawley	Fuel oil	Corby	Steel coil (ceased)

Yard/siding(s)	Inwards from	Traffic	Outwards to	Traffic
MARGAM (cont)	Hardendale	Lime	Dee Marsh (Shotton) (BS)	Steel coil
	Lackenby	Steel	Ebbw Vale	Hot-rolled steel coil
	Warrington/ Newport/Cardiff Tidal	'Enterprise'	Lackenby	Steel
			Llanwern	Imported coal from Grange Sidings (near Margam)
			Llanwern/Ebbw Vale	Steel
			Round Oak/Worcester	Cold-rolled steel coil
			Scunthorpe	Steel
			Shotton (BS)	Hot-rolled steel coil
			Swansea Docks (Burrows Sidings)	Steel slabs
			Swindon	Cold reduced steel coil
			Trostre	Hot-rolled steel coil

Margam's Knuckle Yard is seen on 16 July 1997, on the down side of the South Wales main line between Pyle and Port Talbot Parkway. It was the collecting point for steel traffic to and from Port Talbot. Nearby are Grange coal terminal, Abbey Works, former sorting/holding sidings, and the locomotive inspection depot. When opened, in 1960, the yard was one of the largest and most modern hump yards in the country. In this view, looking west, No 60041 heads 6B82 to Ebbw Vale. *P. D. Shannon*

Approaching Abergavenny station from the south is No 60036 *Sgurr Na Ciche* with a train of BLA wagons carrying loaded steel coil from Margam to Dee Marsh on 3 August 1995.

Above Part of Alexandra Dock Junction Yard, west of Newport on the down side, is seen from an HST on the South Wales main line on 3 August 1995.

Below Looking back towards Newport, No 37889 leaves Alexandra Dock Junction Yard with 6B61, the 0930 to Cardiff Canton, on 28 August 1998. The principal yard for sorting South Wales 'Enterprise' traffic, it was also the 'gateway' to Newport Docks. The line to Machen and Ebbw Vale is visible on the left. *P. D. Shannon*

Yard/siding(s)	Inwards from	Traffic	Outwards to	Traffic
MILFORD HAVEN (Waterston and Robeston)			Albion	Petroleum (ceased 1995)
			Bedworth	Petroleum (ceased 1995)
			Heathfield (Newton Abbot) (W)	Petroleum (ceased 1995)
			Kingsbury	Petroleum (ceased 1995)
			Theale (R)	Murco petroleum
			Westerleigh (R)	Murco petroleum
MOSTYN DOCKS (Warwick Chemicals)	Hull (Saltend)	Acid		
NEWPORT (Alexandra Dock Junction, sorting and staging only)	Burngullow	China clay slurry to Irvine	Barry	Engineers wagons for repairs
			Cadoxton (Chemicals)	Connectrail feeder/trip
			Cardiff Isis Link	Connectrail feeder/trip
			Cardiff Tidal	Connectrail feeder/trip
			Exeter	Connectrail feeder/trip
			Hallen Marsh	Connectrail feeder/trip
			Irvine	China clay slurry from Cornwall
			Swansea (Burrows Sidings)	Connectrail feeder/trip
			Warrington/ Margam	'Enterprise'
			Washwood Heath	Connectrail feeder/trip
			Wembley	Connectrail
NEWPORT (East Usk Yard)	Machen Quarry	Stone ballast		
	Silverdale Colliery	Coal (staging only)		

East Usk Sidings were on the down side of the South Wales main line east of Newport. In this view we are looking west towards Newport on 13 June 1996. These sidings were for the staging of coal and other block trains. The signal box is right of centre, with the quadruple main line to the right.

Penmaenmawr stone loading sidings are on the North Wales coast line by the station, on the up side. Ballast for Railtrack was loaded here for various destinations, including Tuebrook (Liverpool), Gresty Lane (Crewe) and Guide Bridge (Manchester). In this photograph of 16 October 1992, No 60096 heads 25 Roadstone wagons, which are being loaded for Collyhurst Street, Manchester, while No 47358 arrives with empty wagons.

On 22 July 1994 No 37518 is at the head of the 1310 Penmaenmawr to Tuebrook loaded ballast, passing through Llanddulas.

Yard/siding(s)	Inwards from	Traffic	Outwards to	Traffic
ONLLWYN (Opencast/ Washery)			Cardiff (Coastal Sidings)	Containerised coal (Cawoods)
			Steel Supply Briton Ferry	Anthracite duff (very occasional)
			Swansea Docks	Anthracite duff (very occasional)
PANTEG (Steelworks)	Grimsby	Steel (once a month)		
PENMAENMAWR (Associated Road Stone)			Crewe (Gresty Lane)	Stone ballast
			Edge Hill (Liverpool)	Stone ballast
			Guide Bridge	Stone ballast
			Warrington (Arpley)	Stone ballast

Class 60 No 60035 *Florence Nightingale* heads east through Bridgend with iron ore from Port Talbot to Llanwern on 8 August 1994. The loco carries the Goat symbol of Canton depot. Because of the weight of these trains, at one time they were hauled by three Class 37s, two 56s, or a single Class 60 or 59.

Yard/siding(s)	Inwards from	Traffic	Outwards to	Traffic
POINT OF AYR (Colliery)			Fiddlers Ferry PS	Coal
PONTYCYMMER			Jersey Marine (Swansea blending site)	Coal
			Steel Supply	Coal
PORT TALBOT DOCKS			Llanwern	Imported iron ore
ROBESTON (see Milford Haven)				
SWANSEA (Burrows Sidings/Docks)	Cardiff	Tidal Steel bars	Newport	Connectrail
	Coed bach	Coal containers	Warrington/Cardiff/ Mossend	'Enterprise'
	Coed bach	Anthracite duff		
	Halewood and Dagenham	Auto components		
	Margam	Steel slabs		
	Newport	Connectrail		
	Onllwyn	Anthracite duff		
	Various	Wagons for repair		
	Warrington/Cardiff/ Mossend	'Enterprise'		

Swansea Burrows Sidings were on the South Wales main line, accessed from the down side between Briton Ferry and Neath. These sidings were the collecting point for traffic to and from Swansea Docks; they were spread over a wide area and included sidings for the Ford Motor Company, Gower Chemicals and King's Dock. On 28 August 1998, looking north, No 60030 waits with loaded coal from Brynteg, having entered the system via Neath & Brecon Junction, before heading east to Aberthaw Power Station. *P. D. Shannon*

Yard/siding(s)	Inwards from	Traffic	Outwards to	Traffic
SWANSEA (Jersey Marine)	Pontycymmer	Coal	Aberthaw PS	Coal (ceased 1995, expected to restart 1996)
TOWER (Colliery)			Aberthaw PS	Coal (ceased 1995, expected to restart 1996)
TROSTRE (Steelworks)	Llanwern Port Talbot	Hot-rolled steel coil Hot-rolled steel coil	Westhoughton Wisbech Worcester	Tin plate Tin plate Tin plate
VALLEY			Sellafield via Llandudno Junction	Nuclear waste flasks

WATERSTON (see Milford Haven)

Passing Radyr station on 2 September 1994, Class 56 No 56053 *Sir Morgannwg Ganol/County of Mid Glamorgan* heads south with loaded coal from Tower Colliery, subsequently the only deep pit open in Wales, en route to Aberthaw Power Station. The loco carries the Goat symbol of Canton depot.

Class 31s were also used on nuclear flask trains, and on 19 July 1996 No 31534 is about to pass the signal box at Abergele & Pensarn with the Valley to Sellafield service. The porter's trolley on the near platform implies that the station was manned at that time.

Loco depots, stabling and fuelling points, 1995

CANTON (CF), at Cardiff, was the major depot and part of Transrail (based at Crewe), which was one of the three principal freight operating companies in the UK. The depot had an allocation of approximately 150 main-line and shunting locomotives, which were required almost entirely for freight traffic, and not only in South Wales – the depot was the 'home base' for a number of locomotives out-based at St Blazey (Cornwall), Springs Branch (Wigan), Bescot, Buxton and Motherwell. In addition to these main-line locomotives, Canton was responsible for shunting locomotives out-based at Barry, Newport, Margam, Pantyffynnon*, St Blazey, Exeter, and Laira (Plymouth).

Main line locomotives allocated to Canton for freight working were of three Classes – 37, 56 and 60. In addition there was a Class 47 belonging to Rail Express Systems, together with Class 08 and 09, and one 97, shunting locos. With the exception of one Class 08 shunter, which belonged to the Cardiff Railways TOU, all were all operated by Transrail.

In a separate part of the Canton complex, Regional Railways had an important presence where it serviced a fleet of more than 120 diesel multiple units (DMUs), which were primarily for working services out of Cardiff, not only for local operation but with a wide range of destinations including Manchester, Liverpool, Holyhead and Brighton, as well as West Wales. In addition the depot also supplied units for operation around Bristol, Exeter and the South West of England.

The Regional Railways DMUs based at Canton were split between four different classes – 143, 150, 153 and 158. Of the Class 143s, three were owned by Mid-Glamorgan CC, three by West Glamorgan CC, and one by South Glamorgan CC.

In Wales, Canton units stabled overnight at Rhymney, Treherbert, Carmarthen and Holyhead. Main-line locomotives were stabled at Godfrey Road (Newport), Margam and at Barry.

The steam depot on the site closed in September 1962 and a purpose-built diesel depot was erected where the roundhouse once stood. The locomotive side of the depot closed in 2004 and work was transferred to Margam.

HOLYHEAD (HD) was the only refuelling point in North Wales and had no allocation of locomotives or DMUs. The InterCity 125 Class 43s on the Euston to Holyhead services were allocated to Longsight in Manchester, having to return there for maintenance. The Class 37s that worked the Birmingham/Crewe to Bangor/Holyhead trains were owned by Transrail, allocated to Crewe (CD), while the DMUs working the Manchester to Llandudno or Holyhead services were normally from Newton Heath (NH), Manchester, as were the units working the Llandudno to Blaenau Ffestiniog and Llandudno to Holyhead services. Units were stabled overnight at Holyhead and Llandudno Junction.

The only DMUs running into North Wales that were allocated within Wales were those operating the one daily direct service between Holyhead and Cardiff, which was a Canton Class 158. The units that operated the Bidston to Wrexham Central service were from Newton Heath, Manchester, but could be refuelled at Chester – these were normally Class 153s or 142s.

* The anthracite coal traffic from Cwmmawr opencast disposal point ceased at the end of March 1996, thus ending the stabling at Pantyffynnon and Landore of the Class 08/9 shunting locomotives that had the special cut-down cabs for working on the branch.

Cardiff Canton Depot, seen on 3 August 1995 looking west from a passing HST, held locomotives of Classes 08, 37, 47 and 56. On the far left is the DMU servicing area with a Class 158 visible. Built on the site of the old steam shed, the depot opened in 1964; the locomotive side subsequently closed in 2004.

The second view, taken on the same occasion, shows the west end of the depot. The depot symbol was a Goat.

Main-line locomotives based at Canton were stabled at Godfrey Road (Newport). On 3 October we see a line-up of Class 37s and 47s, taken from the west end of the 'island' platform.

In the second view of the stabling point, taken from the road at the west of station, Nos 47362 and 37229 are in the foreground.

Above This is Holyhead Depot on 18 May 1993, looking towards the station (beyond the bridge). On the right-hand side can be seen an 'open-ended' building, erected primarily to muffle the sound when HSTs were being refuelled. A Class 08 shunter can be glimpsed on the left-hand side beyond the signal box. The old depot building was immediately to the right of the rear of the signal box.

Below At Holyhead on 17 February 1995 Class 37 No 37421 *The Kingsman* has run round its train, which it has brought in from Crewe. Nos 37418 and 37408 *Loch Rannoch* are stabled by the small building mentioned in the previous caption.

A steam shed at Holyhead had been located close by from 1861 and closed to steam in 1966, although it continued to service diesel locos until about 1990 and was subsequently demolished.

LANDORE (LE), at Swansea, had a small allocation of three Class 08 shunting locos, which were under the control of the Great Western TOU. In addition there were up to a further three 08s that, although allocated to Canton, were stabled at Landore – these had specially cut down cabs and were fitted with headlights for working the Cwmmawr branch (see footnote on page 33). The depot serviced and repaired Class 43 Intercity 125 HSTs and Rail Express Systems Class 47s. It was also a re-fuelling point. The steam shed had closed in 1961 and a purpose-built diesel depot was established on the site in 1963.

MACHYNLLETH (MN) Traction & Maintenance Depot also had no allocation but carried out routine maintenance of DMUs, which were based at Tyseley (Birmingham) – Classes 153 and 156 – and Norwich Crown Point – Class 158s. The depot had refuelling facilities. Two units were stabled overnight at Pwllheli in order to operate the early-morning services. A steam shed had been on the site since 1863, but it closed to steam in 1966 and was given over to the servicing of DMUs. (In 2007 a new depot was opened for servicing Arriva Trains West Class 158s.)

MARGAM (MG). This depot/Loco Inspection Point and refuelling point had no locomotives allocated to it, and operated under Canton.

In the first of these two photographs of Landore Depot taken from an HST on 4 April 1996, an unidentified Class 47 in Res livery stands with a parcels train, while only a Class 08 shunter is visible in the second. The depot was built in 1963 on the site of the old steam shed.

Above Part of Machynlleth Depot is seen from the end of the up station platform, looking east on 9 May 1996. It was originally a steam shed, which closed in 1966 and was thereafter used as a DMU maintenance depot.

Below This longer-distance view from near the station shows the small yard at Machynlleth, with fuel storage tanks on the right. A new depot was built in 2007, which will be used primarily for maintenance of the Arriva Trains Wales fleet of Class 158s; it was opened on 13 August 2007.

Above Once again taken from a passing HST, this view of Margam depot on 4 April 1996 shows representatives of Classes 37 and 56 bearing the Transrail 'T' logo. The depot opened in 1964 and remains active.

Below Photographed a little further west on the same day, this group of locomotives includes a Class 37 and several Class 56s.

Pool codes, winter 1995

Each loco was allocated into a specific Pool, as follows:

HLSV	Cardiff Railways TOU	Canton Class 08s
LNAK	Transrail	Canton Class 60s (South Wales)
LNBK	Transrail	Canton Class 56s (South Wales)
LNCF	Transrail	Canton Classes 08, 09 and 97
LNCK	Transrail	Canton Class 37/7 (South Wales)
LNDK	Transrail	Canton Class 37/0 and 37/4 (Departmental and on hire to Regional railways South Wales & West for passenger trains)
LNHK	Transrail	Canton Class 37/9s
LNLK	Transrail	Canton Class 37/5s (St Blazey)
LNSK	Transrail	Canton Class 37/0s (Sandite-fitted)
LWAK	Transrail	Canton Class 60s (North West)
LWBK	Transrail	Canton Class 56s (Midlands and North West)
LWCK	Transrail	Canton Class 60 (Buxton)
PWLO	Carriage & Traction Co Ltd	Canton Class 47s
HJSE	Great Western TOU	Landore Class 08s (HST pilot and High Street/ Maliphant Carriage Sidings)

Summary of units and locomotives

DMUs

Class 143	25*
Class 150	41
Class 153	18
Class 158	39
Total units	**123**

* Three owned by Mid-Glamorgan CC, three by West Glamorgan CC and one by South Glamorgan CC

Shunting locomotives

Class 08	1, Cardiff Valleys TOU
	18, Transrail
Class 09	7, Transrail
Class 97	2, Transrail

Locomotives

Main-line locos allocated to Canton (Transrail)

	South Wales	Bescot/Wigan/ Buxton
Class 60	13	21
Class 56	15	26
Class 37	15	25
Class 47		1 (Rail Express Systems)

Total locomotives   **144** (as at mid-1995)

Wagon repairs were carried out at Barry and at Cathays.

British Rail stations in Wales, 1995

At the end of 1995 there were 212* stations open in Wales. These varied from the largest and busiest, Cardiff Central, to tiny single-platform halts such as Sugar Loaf on the Central Wales line, where trains stopped only on request.

At first glance, a number of stations, particularly in North Wales, had retained the size and appearance of a much busier era – Llandudno and Rhyl are examples – but on closer examination it was evident that only a small proportion of the track and platform accommodation was being used. Aberystwyth in Mid Wales retained platforms in excess of operational requirements and the large 'island' platform at Pontypridd, with its various buildings, also reflected a period of greater activity.

During the 1980s and 1990s many new stations were opened, particularly in South Wales on the Valley Lines, as well as on the main line. Some occupied the sites of previously closed stations while some were in new places, to cater for communities that had grown in more recent times. In North Wales new stations were built at Conwy (where the previous station closed in 1966), at Llanfairfechan in the late 1980s, when the old station was demolished to make way for the construction of the A55 Expressway, and at Llanrwst, in a position closer to the town centre. In many instances a considerable part of the funding for these new stations came from local government sources, as well as the European Regional Development Fund and Projects of Regional and National Importance. To facilitate development of a new shopping area, the line to Wrexham Central was cut back by a short distance and a replacement station built.

In South Wales a number of stations were designated as 'Park & Ride' in an effort to encourage motorists to use public transport. Where towns and villages were not served by rail, new initiatives brought about bus services linked specifically to train times. There were plans for more new stations – Baglan on the South Wales main line opened on 2 June 1996 and serious consideration had been given to the re-introduction of passenger services on the freight-only line from Barry, opening stations near Rhoose, to serve Cardiff airport, Gileston, St Athan and terminating at Llantwit Major, but in February 1996 it was announced that the plan had been abandoned. (Later, stations at Rhoose and Llantwit Major were opened in 2005 on the Vale of Glamorgan line between Barry and Bridgend when passenger services re-commenced.) Another possibility was the return of passenger services from Newport to Ebbw Vale (also proceeding in 2007, with six stations planned).

A number of smaller stations are maintained by volunteers from local communities. Dolau on the Central Wales line has won awards in 'Best Unstaffed Station in Wales' and 'Wales in Bloom' competitions. At Llandybie the local County Primary School staff and pupils help to keep the station in excellent order, and Llanwrtyd Wells station has undergone landscaping and has new cast iron signs and a picnic area, thanks to the local Action Group.

Llandrindod Wells station was restored to its Victorian state in 1990, and at Llanfair PG on Anglesey Edinburgh Woollen Mills spent £250,000 on the restoration of the station building, converting it into a museum and tourist attraction. Architecturally some fine examples of more ambitious and prosperous times survive. The grandiose frontage of Aberystwyth station

* Including Knighton (where the station is actually in England, although the town is in Wales) and counting Shotton as two stations.

disguised the fact that a single platform sufficed for operational needs. In the north, several of the Francis Thomson-designed buildings, dating back to the mid-19th century, remain in use, including Bangor and Flint.

It is perhaps overlooked that the famous engineer, Isambard Kingdom Brunel, was responsible for the design of a number of stations in Wales, examples being at Chepstow, Pantyffynnon and Bridgend.

The large station building at Machynlleth has been restored and several stations have been given external 'face-lifts', together with new entrance halls, such as Cardiff Central, Newport and Bridgend. Similarly, in North Wales Colwyn Bay and Holyhead have been modernised, while Rhyl has undergone restoration and at Abergele & Pensarn £73,000 was spent on renovating the forecourt. Alternative uses for station buildings not required for railway use include small businesses, restaurants and private homes.

The new stations built in the 1980s and 1990s are normally very basic structures – often just a platform and simple waiting shelter – undoubtedly in the interests of keeping costs to a minimum. An unusual exception is Conwy where an imaginative approach included most attractive station lamps. A very high percentage of stations had been de-staffed, which led to an increase in vandalism. The presence nearby of a signal box is usually a deterrent in this respect, but gradually these are being reduced in number, as semaphore signals are replaced by modern colour lights, often operated from a distant power box.

Names of lines

Alphaline
This marketing name was used by Regional Railways for selected routes operated by Class 158 units, but not necessarily every service. These included:

Aberystwyth-Birmingham New Street via
  Shrewsbury

Cardiff-Holyhead
Cardiff-Liverpool
Cardiff-Manchester*
Cardiff/Carmarthen-Waterloo
Cardiff-Birmingham*/Nottingham/
  Cleethorpes
Cardiff-Salisbury/Southampton/Portsmouth

* Some services originated at Swansea

Cambrian Lines
Aberystwyth/Pwllheli-Machynlleth/
  Shrewsbury

Central Wales/Heart of Wales Line
Swansea-Shrewsbury via Mid Wales

City Line
Cardiff-Radyr via Ninian Park

Marches Line (also known as North & West
  Line)
Newport-Shrewsbury via Hereford

Swanline
Cardiff-Swansea, RR local services

Valley Lines
Cardiff Central-Aberdare/Coryton/Merthyr/
  Treherbert/Rhymney
Cardiff Central-Barry/Penarth
Cardiff Queen Street-Cardiff Bay

A-Z gazetteer of stations

The stations are included in alphabetical order by the station name as used in the BR all-lines timetable, followed by the Welsh name if different – there are some stations where there is more than one Welsh version. The letter and number reference code refers to the location of the station on the maps on pages 6-10: the letter of the map followed by the grid square reference. The line on which the station is situated is then given, followed by a short history and the date on which the photograph was taken.

ABER   C:D4

Rhymney Valley line
Opened in 1908 as 'Beddau', it was
re-named 'Aber Junction' by the
GWR in 1926, then became 'Aber
Halt' in 1968 before adopting the
present name in the following year.
This view is looking north towards
Llanbradach. *6.10.1994*

ABERCYNON NORTH
(Abercynon Gogledd)   C:C3

Aberdare branch
Looking north towards
Penrhiwceiber, this is a new station,
opened in October 1988 with capital
investment by Mid Glamorgan CC.
2.9.1994

ABERCYNON SOUTH
(Abercynon De)   C:C3

Merthyr Tydfil branch
This is the broad platform looking
north. The station opened in 1840 as
'Navigation House', and was re-
named 'Aberdare Junction' in 1849
and 'Abercynon' in 1896, finally
having 'South' added in 1988 when
Abercynon North was opened. The
line to Aberdare goes off to the left
and that to Merthyr to the right.
2.9.1994

ABERDARE (Aberdâr)   **C:B1**
Terminus of Aberdare branch from Pontypridd
Looking north, we see the new station, opened 3 October 1988 with joint investment capital from Mid Glamorgan CC and the EEC. *8.6.1995*

Looking north from the end of the new station platform, on the right is the previous Aberdare High Level station and ahead the freight-only line to Tower Colliery. *8.6.1995*

ABERDOVEY (Aberdyfi)　　A:C6
Cambrian coast line

Looking north towards Tywyn. This was once the southern terminus of the coast line, before the route to Dovey Junction was constructed. The station dates back to 1867 when it replaced Aberdovey Harbour, which had been opened four years earlier, then a new brick-built station was provided in 1872. In 1909 the old building from the original Pwllheli station was re-erected here. The steps are needed because of the low level of the platform. *2.3.1994*

The station building on the east side of the line is now in private use, hence the modern waiting shelter. *2.3.1994*

ABERERCH   A:B4

Cambrian coast line
Looking east towards Butlins Penychain. The station here dates back to 1884. Re-named 'Abererch Halt' in 1956, the 'Halt' was dropped in 1968. BR applied for permission to close the station in 1994, but it remained open in the Winter timetable of 1995/6 with a note saying that it might close during the currency of the timetable. It was subsequently reprieved by the Department of Transport on the grounds of local hardship and possible damage to the tourist trade. *22.9.1995*

ABERGAVENNY (Y Fenni)
B:H4

Hereford-Newport line
The first view is looking south towards Pontypool from the north end of the up platform, which shows signs that it has been extended in the past. The platform on the left was at one time an 'island'. Opened in 1854, the station was named 'Abergavenny Monmouth Road' between 1950 and 1968, when it reverted to its original name. *8.8.1994*

The station buildings on the up side, for Hereford. *3.8.1995*

ABERGELE & PENSARN (Abergele a Phensarn)   A:E2
North Wales coast line
The view from the east end of the down platform looking west towards Colwyn Bay. The up line was singled some years back, but the down 'through' road remains. The station dates back to the Chester & Holyhead Railway, originally opening in 1848. It was completely rebuilt when the track was quadrupled. *20.9.1995*

In September 1994 renovation was completed of the forecourt and down-side buildings, which included the Booking Office and a Craft Centre, at a cost of £73,000. *20.1.1996*

ABERYSTWYTH   A:C7

Terminus of line from Dovey Junction

The first station here dated back to 1864, but was rebuilt by the GWR in ashlar stone in 1925. In 1964 the line to Carmarthen was closed, and later the Vale of Rheidol narrow gauge railway was diverted to use the redundant BR platform. There is now only one platform in operational use by BR. In 1995 Railtrack announced a multi-million-pound plan to restore the listed station building to include a café, shops and offices, with adjacent railway land to be redeveloped into shops with provision for buses. *27.5.1994*

This view shows the size of the station. The platform on the extreme left is used by the Vale of Rheidol Railway and the DMU is standing at the only platform used by BR. *31.8.1995*

The news-stand during an active period. *27.5.1994*

AMMANFORD (Rhydaman)   **B:E4**
Central Wales line
This is the single platform, looking south towards Pantyffynnon. Opened originally as 'Duffryn' in 1841 as a temporary terminus, it did not become a through station until 1857. In 1889 it became 'Tirydail', then in 1960 'Ammanford & Tirydail', to which the word 'Halt' was added in 1965, before it took the present name in 1973! *25.5.1995*

BAGLAN   **B:F5**
South Wales main line
This new station opened on 3 June 1996 between Port Talbot Parkway and Briton Ferry. In this view looking east, on the right is the M4. *5.6.1996*

BANGOR A:C2

North Wales coast line

This overall view of the station from the west end is looking in the direction of Llanfairfechan. Opened by the Chester & Holyhead Railway in 1848 as the first western terminus of the line, it remained so for only two years, when the line was continued westwards. It has at times been known as 'Bangor (Caerns.)', 'Bangor (Gwynedd)' and sometimes described in certain timetables as 'Bangor for Beaumaris'. As can be seen, the station consisted of two 'island' platforms, but the trackwork has subsequently been rationalised. The two right-hand lines were used for stabling the stock of trains that terminated here. The two centre through lines see only limited use since the Freightliner Terminal at Holyhead closed. *16.6.1994*

Another overall view of the station, this time from the east end, with Belmont Tunnel beyond the signal box. *17.11.1995*

The footbridge at Bangor spans what is now part of the station car park, with the entrance and ticket office on the right, on the up side. *10.11.1993*

BARGOED C:D2
Rhymney Valley line
Opened in 1858, it was known as 'Bargoed & Aber Bargoed' from 1905 to 1924. In this view looking north towards Brithdir, the signal box can be seen beyond the station behind the right-hand semaphore signal. *27.7.1995*

A closer view of the station building, situated on the east side of the line. *27.7.1995*

BARMOUTH (Abermaw)
A:D5
Cambrian coast line
Opening in 1865 as Barmouth Ferry, the station was replaced in 1867 when opened by the A&WC. This photograph of the entrance to the down-side platform was taken from near the promenade looking inland. *12.4.1994*

Looking north towards Pwllheli from the road crossing south of the station, which is the only way across the line, although at one time there was a footbridge at the north end of the station. There is a modern canopy on the down platform. *7.4.1995*

As can be seen from this view from near the north end of the down platform, looking south, there was a bay platform at this end. *12.4.1994*

BARRY (Y Barri)   C:C7

Cardiff Central-Barry Island line
The station opened in 1889. Looking west towards Bridgend, the branch to Barry Island curves away to the left in front of the houses, while the freight-only line to Bridgend (subsequently re-opened for passenger services) is straight ahead. *21.9.1994*

BARRY DOCKS (Dociau'r Barri)   C:C7

Cardiff Central-Barry Island line
Looking south-west towards Barry, the broad expanse of the 'island' platform is dominated by the Barry Dock Office, the original General Offices of the Barry Railway Company and now a Grade II listed building. The station dates back to 1888, when it was known as 'Barry Dock'. An overall canopy was added in 2007. *21.9.1994*

BARRY ISLAND (Ynys y Barri)   C:C7

Terminus of branch from Barry
Opened in 1896 and enlarged by the GWR in 1930, this view of the station is looking towards the end of the line at Barry Pier, to which the last train ran in 1971. Subsequently the station building became a Heritage Centre and HQ for the Vale of Glamorgan Railway Society, which operates a 1¼-mile line with a half-mile inclined branch down to the waterfront. Arriva Trains Wales uses a reduced platform area.

The second picture shows the outside of the station buildings, which were subsequently extensively refurbished. *21.9.1994*

BETWS-Y-COED   A:D3

Blaenau Ffestiniog branch
Looking north towards Llanrwst.
The station was originally opened for
passenger traffic in April 1868 by the
LNWR as 'Bettwys-Y-coed', which
was changed to the present name in
1953, although it is occasionally
described in some timetables as
'Bettws-y-Coed for Capel Curig'.
5.3.1994

The single platform is viewed from
the south end looking north. The
miniature railway and Pullman car
are not part of the BR system but
belong to the Conwy Valley Railway
Museum. The platform length
indicates that at times much longer
trains than the normal were in
operation, probably on excursion
traffic to this popular destination.
5.3.1994

Viewed from the station forecourt,
the buildings now house a café and
shops. *5.3.1994*

BIRCHGROVE (Llwynbedw)   C:D5
Coryton branch
The original station was opened in 1929 by the GWR as 'Birchgrove Halt', but the 'Halt' was dropped by BR in 1969. The station was refurbished in 1987 with capital investment from South Glamorgan CC and other sources in co-operation with Regional Railways, and it is seen here looking west towards Rhiwbina. *6.10.1994*

BLAENAU FFESTINIOG   A:D4
Terminus of branch from Llandudno Junction
In this view of the station looking north towards Roman Bridge, on the left are the platforms for the narrow gauge Ffestiniog Railway, which runs to Porthmadog. The first (temporary) station was opened here in 1879, but closed two years later to be replaced by a second station. The current joint station was opened in 1982 on the site of the old GWR Central station, having attracted close to £1 million of investment from the Welsh Agency, the local authority and a Euro-grant. The line continues on to Trawsfynydd (behind the camera), and up to 1995 had been used for carrying nuclear flasks to and from the power station there. Now this traffic has ceased, it will presumably mean eventual closure of the line south from Blaenau Ffestiniog. *5.3.1994*

BODORGAN   A:B2
North Wales coast line (Anglesey)
This is the view looking north-west
towards Ty Croes. The station was
originally opened in 1849 by the
Chester & Holyhead Railway and
the buildings were designed by
Francis Thompson. *22.6.1993*

BORTH (Y Borth)   A:D6
Dovey Junction-Aberystwyth line
This view of the station is looking
north towards Dovey Junction. When
opened by the Aberystwyth & Welsh
Railway in 1863 it was a terminus,
but this only lasted until the
following year when the line was
fully completed to Aberystwyth.
27.5.1994

The station forecourt and buildings
on the up side. *27.5.1994*

BRIDGEND (Pen-y-bont)   B:F6
South Wales main line
This view of the station is from the down platform looking west towards Pyle. Opened in 1850, the station buildings were designed by I. K. Brunel, and have undergone considerable refurbishment in recent times. Following the subsequent re-commencement of passenger services from Cardiff Central to Bridgend via Barry, the bay on the left is back in regular use. *8.8.1994*

Also looking west, this is the view from the station footbridge. There is a bay on the right-hand side, and in the distance the branch to Maesteg can be seen leaving the main line to the north. *8.8.1994*

BRITHDIR C:D2
Rhymney Valley line
The simple platform and waiting shelter are seen looking north-west towards Tir-Phil. Called 'George Inn' when opened in 1871, the station received its current title in 1891. The disused southbound platform can be seen on the right. *27.7.1995*

BRITON FERRY (Llansawel)
B:F5
South Wales main line
This is a new station, and as can be seen in this view looking south towards Baglan the platforms are partly staggered. There have been three previous stations called Briton Ferry: the first, opened in 1850, became 'Briton Ferry West' in 1924, and the second, opened in 1895, became 'Briton Ferry East', also in 1924. Both closed in 1935 when the third station was opened by the GWR, which lasted until closure in 1964. The current station opened in June 1994. The holding sidings, used for staging coal and other block trains, are on the right. *9.5.1995*

BUCKLEY (Bwcle) A:G3
Bidston-Wrexham Central line
We are looking south towards Penyffordd. The station was called 'Buckley Junction' when opened by the Great Central in 1890, and re-named to the present title in 1974. *4.6.1993*

BUILTH ROAD   B:G2
Central Wales line
The remaining platform and rather imposing station building are seen looking north towards Llandrindod. The line from Llandrindod opened in 1866 and was extended to Garth the following year. Originally 'Builth Junction', the station was re-named 'Builth Road' in 1889, becoming 'Builth Road High Level' from January 1950 to distinguish it from the Cambrian line station; it finally reverted to the current title in 1969. *12.8.1994*

BUTLINS PENYCHAIN
A:C4
Cambrian coast line
The modernised station is seen looking west towards Abererch. Opened by the GWR in 1933 as 'Penychain Halt', it was re-named 'Penychain' in 1947 but was referred to in the BR timetable of 1995 as 'Butlins Penychain'. The second photograph shows the intricate ramp between the road and platform. *22.9.1995*

BYNEA (Bynie) B:E5
Central Wales line
Opened by the Llanelly Railway in the 1850s, possibly earlier, it was re-named 'Bynea Halt' in 1959 before reverting to the present name ten years later. Here are the basic platforms with waiting shelters, looking west towards Llanelli. *20.5.1995*

CADOXTON (Tregatwg)
C:D7
Cardiff Central-Barry Island line
Opened in 1888 by the Barry Railway, this view of the station looking north-east towards Dinas Powys is from the down platform, which was at one time an 'island'. The nearby Biglis Junction station was opened by the Taff Vale as a terminus in 1890, but was only a temporary affair while a dispute over junction arrangements was sorted out by the two companies. A modern building has been constructed on the up platform. On the right is the low-level line that leads into Barry Docks. *21.9.1994*

CAERGWRLE A:G3
Bidston-Wrexham Central line
Opened in 1873 as 'Bridge End', it was re-named 'Caergwrle Castle' in 1898, then in October 1905 'Caergwrle Castle & Wells', before being simplified to the present name in 1974. We are looking south towards Cefn-y-Bedd. *4.6.1993*

CAERPHILLY (Caerffili)　C:D4
Rhymney Valley line
In this view of the station looking north-west towards Aber, the station entrance and buildings are at the town end, on the down (Cardiff) platform. The first station, opened in 1858, was re-sited to the present one in 1871, and extended in 1913 from two to four platforms, with a bay at the Cardiff end. Rationalised in the 1960s to two platforms, the others eventually became part of the bus station. In 1989 improvements were commenced at a reported cost of £200,000. *6.10.1994*

CAERSWS　A:E6
Shrewsbury-Aberystwyth line
Looking from the road crossing north-west towards Machynlleth, the signal box is to the right, off picture, close to the east end of the platform. The station was opened in 1863 by the Newtown & Machynlleth Railway. *23.11.1993*

CALDICOT B:I6

Gloucester-Newport line
This is the completely modernised station looking west towards Severn Tunnel Junction. Originally known as 'Caldicot Halt' when opened by the GWR in September 1932, it was re-named to the present title in May 1969. *21.3.1995*

CARDIFF BAY (Bae Caerdydd) C:D6

Terminus of branch from Cardiff Queen Street
Opened originally as 'Bute Dock', then 'Cardiff Docks' in the early 1840s, it was re-named 'Cardiff Bute Road' by the GWR in 1924 before taking its present title in September 1994. This is the single platform looking towards the buffers. *2.9.1994*

Viewed from outside, the former Taff Vale station building is much as it was when originally built, and now has Listed Building status. *28.11.1995*

CARDIFF CENTRAL (Caerdydd Canolog)   C:D5
South Wales main line
The station consisted of three 'island' platforms, with six platform faces, seen here looking west. To the right are Platforms 1 (off camera) and 2, which are normally used for up trains. When opened in 1850 (enlarged in 1896), it was called simply 'Cardiff', then 'General' was added by the GWR in 1924; it became 'Central' in 1973. *8.8.1994*

We are looking east from the west end of Platforms 6/7, which are used primarily for the various 'Valleys' lines. At one time there was a bay platform at the west end of the left-hand Platforms 3/4. *8.8.1994*

In 1994 a serious fire at Cardiff Central resulted in the partial demolition of one of the buildings, as seen here at the east end of Platforms 3/4, looking west. *8.8.1994*

The imposing entrance, which perpetuates the connection with the Great Western Railway, underwent a 'face-lift' in 1983/4 when the concourse was modernised. *28.11.1995*

CARDIFF QUEEN STREET (Caerdydd Heol y Frenhines)   C:D5
Cardiff Bay-Rhymney Valley line

Looking north towards Heath High Level, there are three platform faces in use. Opened in 1840, the station was refurbished in 1989 and a plaque was unveiled on 15 December 1990 marking the completion of the £600,000 project to improve track and modernise signalling.

The second view shows the modern station entrance at street level. *8.8.1994*

CARMARTHEN
(Caerfyrddin) B:D4
South Wales main line
This overall view of the station was
taken from the east end, where the
line ends. Whether 'through' or
terminating, all trains have to enter
and reverse out of the station. This
was the second station built here and
was opened by the GWR in 1902, the
first dating back to the 1860s. Until
closure in 1956 the Cambrian line
from Aberystwyth came in from the
north.

The second photograph shows the
station approach and buildings, and
the third is the view looking west
along Platform 2 under the canopy.
29.6.1994

CATHAYS   C:D5

Cardiff Queen Street-Radyr line
Opened in October 1983, and seen
looking north-west towards Llandaf,
this was the first new station to be
opened in South Wales for more than
40 years, to serve the University and
office area to the north of the city
centre, with joint funding from South
Glamorgan CC in co-operation with
Regional Railways. *2.9.1994*

CEFN-Y-BEDD   A:G3

Bidston-Wrexham Central line
Looking north towards Caergwrle,
the basic platforms with waiting
shelters can be seen. Opened in 1866
by the Wrexham, Mold & Connah's
Quay Railway, it ultimately came
under the control of the Great
Central, which in turn gave the
LNER its only entry into Wales.
4.6.1993

CHEPSTOW (Cas-gwent)
B:I5

Gloucester-Newport line
The station is seen from the down
platform, looking south towards
Caldicot. Opened in 1850, the
station buildings were designed by
the famous engineer I. K. Brunel.
21.3.1995

CHIRK (Y Waun) A:G4
Chester-Shrewsbury line
Seen looking north towards Ruabon, the station opened in 1848. Nearby is the Kronospan Works, which remained rail-connected although out of use. (Subsequently timber was again being brought in by rail on a regular basis.) *20.8.1993*

CILMERI B:G2/3
Central Wales line
The basic platform and a waiting shelter are seen looking south-east towards Garth. When originally opened in 1867 the station was called 'Cefn-Y-Bedd', and was subsequently re-named 'Cilmery' in 1868, then 'Cilmery Halt' in 1936, receiving its current name in May 1980. *25.6.1994*

CLARBESTON ROAD
B:B4
Carmarthen-Fishguard Harbour line
Looking north-west towards Fishguard Harbour, the basic platforms with waiting shelters are all that remains of a station that replaced the original 1854 one in 1914. The branch to Milford Haven diverges to the west of the station. *25.6.1994*

CLUNDERWEN   B:C4

Carmarthen-Fishguard Harbour line
Looking west towards Clarbeston Road, it can be seen that the platforms are staggered – the down platform can just be seen on the left beyond the trees. When opened in 1854 it was known as 'Narberth Road', then became 'Clynderwen' in 1875, 'Clunderwen Halt' from 1965 to 1969, finally receiving its present name in 1980. *28.6.1994*

COGAN   C:D6

Cardiff Central-Barry Island line
In this view looking north towards Grangetown from the up platform, it can be seen that the platform was once an 'island', and there were at one time exchange sidings between the Barry Railway and the Taff Vale Railway. Opened in 1888, it was originally the terminus of the line from Barry, until it was completed through to Cardiff in 1893. *21.9.1994*

COLWYN BAY (Bae Colwyn)   A:E2

North Wales coast line
The photograph was taken from the end of the down platform looking west towards Llandudno Junction. Opened in 1849 as 'Colwyn', the station was enlarged in 1876 and re-named to the present title. In 1885 the platforms were widened and a new station house and waiting rooms were added. It was completely rebuilt in 1904 when the lines were quadrupled. A new station approach, entrance and booking office opened on the down side in April 1982. *9.7.1993*

CONWY   A:D2
North Wales coast line
Seen looking east towards Llandudno Junction, the station was originally 'Conway' when opened in 1848 by the Chester & Holyhead Railway. Closed in 1966, it re-opened as 'Conwy' in 1987 on a site to the east of the earlier one, following refurbishment at a cost of £200,000 funded with support from Gwynedd CC and the Welsh Office. The platforms are not connected. Note the attractive design of the lights. The station is unmanned and has suffered considerably from vandalism. *17.9.1993*

CORYTON   C:D5
Terminus of branch from Cardiff Queen Street-Caerphilly line
Opened in 1911 as 'Coryton Platform', 'Halt' was added in 1924 before the station became a terminus in 1931, prior to which the line had continued on towards Treforest. It was re-named to its present title in May 1969. The station was refurbished in 1987 with investment from South Glamorgan CC, plus ERDF and PRNI grants, and is seen from the end of the line looking east towards Whitchurch. *6.10.1994*

CRICCIETH (Cricieth)
A:C4

Cambrian coast line
The station, seen here looking east towards Porthmadog, was opened in 1867 by the Aberystwyth & Welsh Coast Railway, later to become part of the Cambrian, which eventually amalgamated with the GWR. The second photograph shows the buildings on the up side, part of which are in use by a TV company.
12.4.1994

CWMBACH   C:B2
Aberdare branch
This new station was built with investment from Mid Glamorgan CC and opened in 1988. It is seen here looking north towards Aberdare.
8.6.1995

CWMBRAN (Cwmbrân)
B:H5
Hereford-Newport line
This overall view of the station is looking north towards Pontypool. Again, this is a new station, opened on 12 May 1986 with investment from Mid Glamorgan CC. The first station here opened in 1880 but closed only two years later, being replaced by a second one, which lasted until closure in 1962. *8.8.1994*

CYNGHORDY   **B:F3**
Central Wales line
This is the view looking south towards Llandovery. Cynghordy Viaduct lies some 300 yards to the north. Originally opened in 1868, it was announced in April 1996 that the station had been selected to test the first solar-powered station light, which would be funded by the Centre for Alternative Technology and the Railway Development Society. *25.6.1994*

DANESCOURT   **C:D5**
Cardiff Central-Radyr (City Line)
This view of the station is from the nearby road bridge, looking north towards Radyr. A new station, opened in 1987, it received investment assistance from South Glamorgan CC and grants from ERDF and PRNI in co-operation with Regional Railways. *12.4.1995*

DEGANWY A:D2
Llandudno branch
This is the only station on the branch between Llandudno Junction and Llandudno, and is seen here looking towards Llandudno. The main buildings were on the up side. At the far end of the platform on the left can be seen the signal box controlling the level crossing. The station was opened in 1868 as 'Deganway', receiving its present name in 1882. *9.7.1993*

Aberconwy BC had granted planning permission for development of the station buildings as a public house and restaurant, but in June 1995 cracks appeared in the building, which had to be shored up, and in March 1996 it was demolished. *30.12.1993*

DINAS POWYS   C:D6
Cardiff Central-Barry Island line
We are looking north-east towards Eastbrook. Opened as 'Dinas Powis' in 1888, it was renamed 'Dynas Powis' before being changed to the preferred spelling in 1980. *21.9.1994*

DINAS RHONDDA   C:B3
Treherbert line
Looking north towards Tonypandy, there is just a single platform with a basic waiting shelter. On the extreme left the old up-side platform can just be seen. The station dates back to 1886 when it replaced nearby Pandy, but was closed in 1917. It re-opened in 1919 as 'Dinas Rhondda', but is sometimes referred to simply as 'Dinas'. *12.4.1995*

DINGLE ROAD (Heol Dingle)   C:D6
Cardiff Central-Penarth line
Seen here looking south towards Penarth, the station has been variously known as 'Dingle Road Platform' when opened in 1904, then 'Dingle Road Halt' in 1922, before becoming 'Dingle Road' in 1969. *21.9.1994*

DOLAU B:G2
Central Wales line
Dating back to 1865, the station changed name to 'Dolau Halt' in 1965 but reverted to 'Dolau' in 1969. It has won many awards for 'Best Unstaffed Station in Wales', 'Wales in Bloom', etc, as well as a special award for exceptional community involvement, and the reason is clearly evident in this view of the platform looking south towards Pen-y-bont. *12.8.1994*

DOLGARROG A:D2
Blaenau Ffestiniog branch
The modest platform and waiting shelter are seen looking north towards Tal-y-Cafn. The halt was opened in 1916 and closed in 1964, but re-opened in 1965. *5.3.1994*

DOLWYDDELAN A:D3
Blaenau Ffestiniog branch
Opened in 1879, it was the only 'island' platform on the branch, and was known at times as 'Dolyddelen', but subsequently settled to the present spelling. In 2006 the station, seen here looking north-east towards Pont-y-Pant, won an award for 'The UK's Most Enhanced Community Station' in recognition of the work of two local groups to improve the station environment. *5.3.1994*

DOVEY JUNCTION
(Cyffordd Dyfi)   **A:D6**
Junction of lines from Aberystwyth and Pwllheli

The first photograph shows the Aberystwyth platform, looking towards Borth. Originally opened in 1867 as 'Glan Dovey Junction', it was re-named to the present title in 1904. Purely a rail junction without road access, the station is at sea-level and susceptible to flooding at times of unusually high tides.

The second photograph is of the disused part of the Aberystwyth/ Machynlleth platform, looking towards the latter and the modernised station beyond.

Finally, the third view is of the Pwllheli/Machynlleth platform, again looking towards the latter and showing the modern waiting shelter. *2.3.1994*

DYFFRYN ARDUDWY   A:C5
Cambrian coast line
This is the view looking north towards Llanbedr. The station opened in 1867 as 'Dyffryn' and was re-named 'Dyffryn-on-Sea' in 1924 before taking the present name in 1948. *12.4.1994*

EASTBROOK   C:D6
Cardiff Central-Barry Island line
Seen from the station footbridge, looking north-east towards Cogan, this new station was opened on 24 November 1986 at a cost of £160,000, funded jointly by South Glamorgan CC and grants from ERDF and PRNI in co-operation with Regional Railways. *21.9.1994*

FAIRBOURNE (Y Friog)
A:D5

Cambrian coast line
Named 'Barmouth Ferry' when
opened in 1865, the station closed in
1867. It re-opened on the site of the
earlier station, re-named to its
present title, in 1897, and is seen here
looking south towards Llwyngwril.
27.5.1994

FAIRWATER (Y Tyllgoed)
C:D5

Cardiff Central-Radyr (City Line)
Seen looking north towards
Danescourt, the station opened in
October 1987 with investment by
South Glamorgan CC and grants
from ERDF and PRNI working with
Regional Railways. *12.4.1995*

FERNHILL   **C:B2**
Aberdare branch
Looking north towards Cwmbach,
this new station opened on 3 October
1988 with investment by Mid-
Glamorgan CC. *8.6.1995*

FERRYSIDE (Glanyfferi)

B:D4

Swansea-Carmarthen line
The station dates back to 1852 and these two views are looking south towards Kidwelly, with the signal box and crossing beyond and showing the basic platforms with waiting shelters, and looking north towards Carmarthen. *25.5.1995*

FFAIRFACH   **B:E4**

Central Wales line
Opened originally in 1857, the station was later re-named 'Ffairfach Halt', but reverted to the existing title in 1969; it is seen here looking south towards Llandybie. *2.7.1994*

FISHGUARD HARBOUR (Porthladd Abergwaun or Harbwr Abergwaun)   B:B3
Terminus of line from Carmarthen
The station was opened by the GWR in 1906. In the background is an Irish ferry bound for Rosslare.
  The second view shows the station looking towards Clarbeston Road. *27.5.1993*

FLINT (Fflint)   **A:F2**
North Wales coast line

Opened in 1848 by the Chester & Holyhead Railway, this is the view looking north-west towards Prestatyn. The down platform (left) was extended in 1979. The waiting room on the other platform was built in 1883. At one time there was a platform-mounted signal box on the up side. *16.7.1993*

The original down-side station building, designed by Francis Thompson, viewed from the forecourt. The near part used at one time as a public house appropriately called 'The Sidings'. *7.3.1996*

GARTH   B:G3
Central Wales line
The station dates back to 1867, and we are looking south towards Llangammarch; the remains of the northbound platform can be seen on the right. Curiously it was some time before '(Powys)' was added to the station name to distinguish it from the other station of the same name in Mid Glamorgan. *25.6.1994*

GARTH (MID GLAMORGAN)   B:F5
Maesteg branch
Seen looking north towards Maesteg Ewenny Road, this new station opened on 28 September 1992 with capital investment by Mid Glamorgan CC. *28.6.1995*

GILFACH FARGOED
C:D2
Rhymney Valley line
The station dates back to 1908, when it opened as 'Gilfach Fargoed Halt'; subsequently the word 'Halt' was dropped by BR. Seen looking north towards Bargoed, in the Summer 1995 timetable is was a 'request stop'. *27.7.1995*

GLAN CONWY A:E2
Blaenau Ffestiniog branch
This view of the station is looking north towards Llandudno Junction. Called 'Llansantffraid' when opened in 1863, it became 'Glan Conway' shortly afterwards in 1865. Closed by BR in 1964, it re-opened in 1970 and was re-named to the present title in 1980. *5.3.1994*

GOWERTON (Tre-gwyr) B:E5
Swansea-Carmarthen line
Opening in 1854 as Gower Road, at one time it became Gowerton North, but finally received the present name in 1968. The photograph, looking towards Llanelli, clearly illustrates the reduction to single track, with the redundant platform on the right. *25.5.1995*

GRANGETOWN C:D6
Cardiff Central-Penarth line
This view is looking north along the very wide 'island' platform towards Cardiff. At one time there was a building with a canopy on each side. Opened in 1882, for a period the station name carried the suffix '(South Glamorgan)' to separate it from a station of the same name in Cleveland, which subsequently closed. *21.9.1994*

GWERSYLLT   A:G3
Bidston-Wrexham Central line
The station opened in 1866 as 'Gwersyllt & Wheatsheaf', which was changed to the present name in 1959. A northbound train arrives from Wrexham General. *4.6.1993*

HARLECH   A:C4
Cambrian coast line
The station is seen here from the Castle ramparts looking north-west, clearly showing the length of the platforms, and that the station is a passing place on this single line. *31.8.1991*

A close-up of the down-side buildings at Harlech. The station was originally opened by the Cambrian Railways in 1867. In 1995 it was 'adopted' by the local school and the pupils improved the appearance with tubs of flowers and shrubs.
12.4.1994

HAVERFORDWEST
(Hwlffordd)   B:B4
Clarbeston Road-Milford Haven line
This view towards Clarbeston Road shows the main station buildings on the up side. With a history dating back to the opening of the line in 1854, the station was described in some timetables as 'Haverfordwest for St David's'. The second photograph shows the station building from the approach road.
1.7.1994

HAWARDEN (Penarlâg)
A:G3
Bidston-Wrexham Central line
The station was opened by the
Wrexham, Mold & Connah's Quay
Railway in 1890, and is seen here
looking north towards Shotton. Later
the line became part of the Great
Central Railway, then, in 1923, the
LNER, being the only foothold the
latter had in Wales. *4.6.1993*

HAWARDEN BRIDGE (Pont Penarlâg)   **A:G2**
Bidston-Wrexham Central line
Beyond the platforms in this view of
the station looking north towards
Neston can be seen Dee Marsh
Junction signal box, which controls
access to Shotton Steelworks. The
station was built originally for
workers at John Summers, and
opened in 1924 as 'Hawarden Bridge
Halt', but the word 'Halt' was
subsequently dropped. The nearby
bridge over the River Dee was
opened by the wife of the Rt Hon W.
E. Gladstone on 3 August 1889.
19.7.1994

HEATH HIGH LEVEL (Lefel Uchel y Mynydd Bychan)
C:D5
Rhymney Valley line
This view of the station is looking
north towards Llanishen. Dating
back to 1915 and known at one time
as 'Heath Halt High Level', the word
'Halt' was subsequently dropped.
6.10.1994

HEATH LOW LEVEL (Lefel Isel y Mynydd Bychan)   C:D5
Coryton branch
Seen here looking north-west towards Ty Glas, the original station opened in 1911, and was known for a time as 'Heath Halt (Cardiff)', later 'Heath Halt Low Level', before the present name was adopted. It was refurbished in 1987 with financial investment by South Glamorgan CC with grants from ERDF and PRNI. *6.10.1994*

HENGOED   C:D3
Rhymney Valley line
The original station was opened in 1858, becoming 'Hengoed & Maescwmmer' in 1905, then 'Hengoed Low Level', and finally back to the original name in May 1968. We are looking north towards Pengam. *27.7.1995*

HOLYHEAD (Caergybi)   A:B2
Terminus of North Wales coast line (Anglesey)
The station is divided by the approach road, as can be seen in this photograph. Platform 1 is to the left and the others to the right. The original and temporary station was opened by the Chester & Holyhead Railway in 1848, replaced by a new station three years later. The existing station is the third, dating back to 1866. The first hotel opened in 1880, surviving until 1951. The station underwent considerable refurbishment in 1989. *10.11.1993*

The second picture shows the west side of the station, with Platform 1 and the new Ferry Terminal buildings on the right and to the left the covered footbridge leading to the town. *17.11.1995*

At Holyhead on the same day, on the right is the new vehicle entrance to the departure area for the ferries to Ireland; at one time this was a Freightliner Terminal, which closed in 1991. On the left Nos 156428+424 stand at Platform 4 with the 'Irish Mancunian'. *17.11.1995*

A close-up of the end of Platform 4 and the older part of the station on the east side. *17.11.1995*

HOPE (Yr Hôb)   **A:G3**
Bidston-Wrexham Central line
This view of the station is looking north towards Penyffordd. Originally opened in 1866 as 'Caergwrle', it was re-named 'Hope Village' in 1899. The name changed again in 1974 to its present title. *4.6.1993*

JOHNSTON   B:B4

Clarbeston Road-Milford Haven line
The single remaining platform is seen looking north towards Haverfordwest. Dating back to 1856, the station became 'Milford Road' in 1859 before reverting to its present name in 1863. It was subsequently given the suffix '(Pembroke)', but that is no longer necessary. *27.6.1994*

KIDWELLY (Cydweli)
B:D5

Swansea-Carmarthen line
The firstphotograph was taken from the road crossing, looking north through the station towards Ferryside. There has been a station here since 1852.

The second view is looking south towards Pembrey & Burry Port, with the level crossing and signal box at the far end of the station. *25.5.1995*

KILGETTY (Cilgeti) B:C5
Pembroke Dock branch
Looking north towards Narberth, the single platform with basic waiting shelter can be seen. Originally opened in 1866 by the Pembroke & Tenby Railway as 'Kilgetty & Begelly', the name was simplified to the current one by the GWR in 1901. *29.6.1994*

KNIGHTON (Trefclawdd) B:H1
Central Wales line
It must be stated that, while the town is in Wales, the station is actually just over the border in England (the only such exception in this book!). The first picture is looking south, with the main station buildings on the left, the town side – the exterior is seen in the second photograph. Opened in 1861, the line on to Knucklas was opened for mineral traffic in 1862, while from Knighton to Llandrindod Wells was formally opened in October 1865. Re-named 'Knighton Halt' in 1965, and described in some timetables as 'Knighton for Presteigne', it reverted to the current title in 1969. A new passing loop was installed in 1965. *12.8.1994*

KNUCKLAS (Cnwclas)
B:H1
Central Wales line
Looking south towards Llangynllo, we see the single platform with waiting shelter – good use has been put to old tyres for flower beds. The station dates back to 1865, was re-named 'Knucklas Halt' in 1956, but reverted to the present name in 1969. Close by is the 13-arch viaduct, built in 1865. *12.8.1994*

LAMPHEY (Llandyfái)
B:B5
Pembroke Dock branch
The single platform with waiting shelter are seen looking east towards Manorbier. The station was opened in 1863 by the Pembroke & Tenby Railway. *27.6.1994*

LISVANE & THORNHILL (Llysfaen a Draenan Pen-y-Graig) **C:D4**
Rhymney Valley line
This new station opened in November 1985, with investment from South Glamorgan CC and Regional Railways. Seen here looking north towards Caerphilly, it replaced the nearby and hardly used Cefn-onn station. *6.10.1994*

LLANABER   A:D5

Cambrian coast line
The view is looking north towards
Talybont. Opened as 'Llanaber Halt'
in 1914, the name was simplified 54
years later in 1968 to the current
one. *12.4.1994*

LLANBEDR   A:C5

Cambrian coast line
The photograph was taken looking
north towards Pensarn. Opened in
July 1923 as 'Talwrn Bach Halt', the
station subsequently became 'Talwrn
Bach' in 1968 before the current title
was adopted in 1978. *12.4.1994*

LLANBISTER ROAD   B:H2

Central Wales line
The platform is seen looking south
towards Dolau, with the old station
house on the left. There is a basic
waiting shelter at the far end of the
platform. Opened in 1868, possibly
earlier, it became 'Llanbister Road
Halt' in 1964 before reverting to the
original name five years later.
12.8.1994

LLANBRADACH   C:D4
Rhymney Valley line
Looking south towards Aber, it can be seen that the platforms are staggered but connected by a footbridge. The original station on the site was opened in 1893. *27.7.1995*

LLANDAF   C:D5
Cardiff Queen Street-Radyr line
Llandaf Loop Junction signal box can be seen at the far end of the platform in this view looking north towards Radyr. The station opened in 1840 as 'Llandaff', and was re-named 'Llandaff for Whitchurch' before taking the existing name in 1980. *12.4.1995*

LLANDANWG   A:C4
Cambrian coast line
The tiny platform, seen here looking south towards Pensarn, was opened by the GWR as 'Llandanwg Halt' in 1929; the 'Halt' suffix was dropped in 1968. The second picture gives a further idea of the remoteness of the station. *12.4.1994*

LLANDECWYN   A:D4

Cambrian coast line
Here is another small platform in quite an isolated situation, looking north towards Penrhyndeudraeth. Originally opened in the mid-1930s as 'Llandecwyn Halt', it acquired its current name in 1968. BR applied for closure in 1994, but following a public enquiry the Department of Transport refused permission.

The second view shows the rear of the simple wooden platform.
12.4.1994

LLANDEILO   B:E4

Central Wales line
Looking north-west towards Llangadog, the closed brick-built signal box remained in situ at the north end of the Swansea platform, but has subsequently been demolished. Opened in 1857, the station was once the junction with the line to Carmarthen. Its name was changed from 'Llandilo' to the present spelling by BR. It remains a crossing place.

The station buildings and signal box had suffered from vandalism and neglect, as seen in the inset, and in March 1996 were demolished. A town bypass was under discussion, which might have meant moving the site of the station, but in 2007 this remained undecided. *2.7.1994*

LLANDOVERY
(Llanymddyfri)   B:F3
Central Wales line
This is the view looking south-west towards Llanwrda. The station dates back to its opening in 1858 by the Vale of Towy Joint Railway, and is a passing place. *25.6.1994*

LLANDRINDOD   B:G2
Central Wales line
The first view is from the south end of the Swansea platform looking north towards Pen-y-Bont. The signal box was moved from a nearby road crossing to the platform and is now a museum. The station opened in 1865, was re-named 'Llandrindod (Wells)' in 1876, the brackets were dropped in 1892, BR added the word 'Halt' in 1968, then it reverted to its present title in 1980. It underwent considerable renovation and 're-Victorianisation' in 1990, and at the time the photo was taken it was the only manned station on the Central Wales line.

The second picture is looking south towards Builth Road. The canopy on the left was once part of the County Council Offices. *5.8.1993*

LLANDUDNO   A:D2
Terminus of branch from Llandudno Junction

The upper picture shows the scale of the station. The first one was opened by the Chester & Holyhead Railway in 1858, but a new five-platform terminus was opened in 1903. The central carriage drive can be seen in the middle of the picture. The station was considerably rationalised in 1978 to reflect the diminished modern-day requirements.

The second picture shows the central carriage drive from outside the station. *17.8.1995*

LLANDUDNO JUNCTION
(Cyffordd Llandudno)   A:D2
North Wales coast line
The station, viewed here from the
east end, is basically two 'islands'
with three platform faces in use, plus
a bay at the west end on the up side.
The yard is on the left-hand side. The
original station was opened in 1858
by the Chester & Holyhead Railway,
but was replaced by the current one
in 1897. *28.1.1994*

This is the view from the other end
of the station looking east, with the
bay platform to the left of centre.
Services from Holyhead to
Llandudno normally used this bay,
and reverse out to take the branch to
Llandudno. *7.7.1995*

The third picture shows the entrance
to the station on the up side of the
line. *30.12.1993*

LLANDYBIE   B:E4
Central Wales line
The platform is seen from the road crossing looking south towards Ammanford. The station was kept tidy by the staff and pupils of Llandybie County Primary School, who were busy the day the photograph was taken. Opened originally in 1857 as 'Llandebie', it took the present title in 1971. *25.5.1995*

LLANELLI (Llanelly)   B:E5
Swansea-Carmarthen line
The station opened in 1852 as 'Llanelly', and the name was changed to the present spelling in 1966; it was modernised in 1979. Trains to and from Swansea for the Central Wales line have to reverse here. The first picture shows the station looking west towards Pembrey & Burry Port, and the second the station frontage and entrance. *25.5.1995*

LLANFAIRFECHAN   A:D2

North Wales coast line
The original station was opened in 1860 but demolished in 1987 to make way for the A55 'Expressway' road, being replaced by the existing station with attractive waiting shelters on each platform. The view is taken from the end of the down platform looking east towards Penmaenmawr. *20.9.1995*

LLANFAIRPWLLGWYNGYLL GOGERYCHWYRNDROBWLL LLANTYSILIOGOGOGOCH

A:C2

North Wales coast line (Anglesey)
In the first picture the station is viewed from the end of the down platform, looking east towards Bangor. Opened in 1848, it survived until 1966 when it was closed; it then re-opened in 1970 before being closed for the second time in 1972 following fire damage to the Britannia Bridge across the Menai Strait. It re-opened again in 1973. In 1994 Edinburgh Woollen Mills, which has a retail outlet close by, renovated the station completely and converted the buildings on the up side into a railway museum and tourist centre. The second picture shows the station building from the car park. (Incidentally, the name translates as 'the Church of St Mary by the whirlpool near the White Hazels near the Church of St Tysilio the Red'.) *22.6.1993*

LLANGADOG   B:E4
Central Wales line
The platform and waiting shelter are seen here looking north-east towards Llanwrda. The station dates back to its opening in 1858 as 'Llangadock'; it was re-named 'Llangadog' in 1958, then 'Halt' was added in 1965 before it reverted to its existing title in 1969. *2.7.1994*

LLANGAMMARCH   B:G3
Central Wales line
The platform is on the west side of the line, as seen in this view looking north towards Garth. Opened in 1867, the station was re-named 'Llangammarch Wells' in 1883, reverting to its current name in 1980. *25.6.1994*

LLANGENNECH   B:E5
Central Wales line
Located near the southerly end of the line, which is double-tracked from Morlais Junction, this view is looking south towards Bynea. The station was opened in 1850 and had the suffix 'Halt' added in 1959 before reverting to its original name ten years later. *25.5.1995*

LLANGYNLLO   B:H1
Central Wales line
In this view looking south towards Llanbister Road, the platform is on the west side of the line. Originally 'Llyncoch' when opened in 1865, it later became 'Llangunllo', then 'Halt' was added in 1965 before it reverted to the current title in 1980. *12.8.1994*

LLANISHEN   C:D4
Rhymney Valley line
The view of this 1871 station is looking north towards Lisvane & Thornhill. *6.10.1994*

LLANRWST A:D3
Blaenau Ffestiniog branch
Looking towards North Llanrwst, this is a new station in a new position, opened in July 1989, in order to bring the railway closer to the town centre. *5.3.1994*

LLANSAMLET B:E5
South Wales main line
Looking east towards Skewen, it can be seen that the platforms are staggered – the down platform can be seen under the bridge. The first station here was opened in 1852, and was closed and replaced by a second station in 1885. It was re-named 'Llansamlet North' in February 1950 before closure in 1964. The present modern station was opened in June 1994. *9.5.1995*

LLANWRDA   B:E4
Central Wales line
The basic platform and waiting shelter are seen here looking north towards Llandovery. Opened to passengers in 1858 as 'Lampeter Road', it was re-named 'Llanwrda' in 1868, and changed again to 'Llanwrda Halt' in 1965, but reverted to the current name in 1969. The second picture is a closer view of the north end of the platform. *2.7.1994*

LLANWRTYD   B:F3
Central Wales line
We are looking east towards Llangammarch. Opened in 1867, the station was re-named 'Llanwrtyd Wells' before reverting to the original name in 1980. *25.6.1994*

The Swansea platform is viewed looking south-west towards Sugar Loaf. A local action group played an important part in restoring the station in 1995, with new cast-iron signs and platform flower-beds. Part of the buildings are leased to a catering concern. *25.6.1994*

LLWYNGWRIL A:C5
Cambrian coast line
Looking north towards Fairbourne, the platform and buildings are on the east side of the line. The station opened as a temporary terminus in 1863 and as a through station in 1865. *27.5.1994*

LLWYNYPIA C:B3
Treherbert line
We are looking north-west towards Ystrad Rhondda, and the platform is on the east side of the line. The station was opened in 1871 as 'Llwynypia & Tonypandy', and re-named to the present title in 1908. *26.4.1995*

MACHYNLLETH　A:D6

Shrewsbury-Aberystwyth line
From the up platform we are looking west towards Dovey Junction. Opened in 1863, the main station buildings were built as the headquarters of the Newtown & Machynlleth Railway. The station underwent considerable restoration from 1993 at a cost of £700,000, financed jointly by Mid Wales Tourism, Development Board for Rural Wales, Railway Heritage Trust and European Regional Developments. The work was completed by 1995 and formally opened on 18 March 1996. The Mid Wales Tourism Office is based here.

The second photograph was taken from the station footbridge, again looking towards Dovey Junction. The station is a passing place.
27.5.1994

The front of the station buildings following refurbishment. *11.4.1995*

MAESTEG   B:F5

Terminus of branch from Bridgend
This new station opened on 28
September 1992 with investment by
Mid Glamorgan CC and the EEC.
The platform is on the town side and
the view is looking north. Beyond the
station a freight-only line continued,
but is currently (2007) out of use.
The first station in the town opened
in 1864, was re-named 'Maesteg
Castle Street' in 1924, and was
closed by BR in 1970. *28.6.1995*

MAESTEG EWENNY ROAD
(Maesteg Heol Ewenny)

B:F5

Maesteg branch
Viewed from a nearby road bridge,
looking north towards Maesteg, this
is also a new station, opened on 26
October 1992, with capital
investment by Mid Glamorgan CC. It
was built 100 yards south of the
former GWR station. *28.6.1995*

MANORBIER (Maenorbyr)

B:B5

Pembroke Dock branch
Seen looking east towards Penally,
over the road crossing, the station
originally opened in 1863 and in
some timetables was described as
'Manorbier for St Florence'.
29.6.1994

MERTHYR TYDFIL (Merthyr Tudful) C:B1
Terminus of branch from Pontypridd
Opened in 1853, at one time the station was known as 'Merthyr High Street', but changed to the present name in 1980. The original Brunel building was demolished in 1971 and replaced by the one pictured. However, in January 1996 a new station was opened 200 yards to the south to allow development of the former site. *2.9.1994*

A later view of the new station from the Pentre-bach end of the platform. *28.2.1996*

MERTHYR VALE
(Ynysowen)   C:C2
Merthyr Tydfil branch
This view of the longish platform
with waiting shelter is looking south
towards Quaker's Yard. The station
dates from 1883. *3.8.1995*

MILFORD HAVEN
(Aberdaugleddau)   B:B5
*Terminus of branch from Clarbeston
Road*
Opened in 1863, the station has been
known variously over the years as
'Milford', 'New Milford' or 'Old
Milford', before settling down to the
current name by 1906/7. The first
picture shows the station approach
road, and the second the platform
looking towards the buffers.
27.6.1994

MINFFORDD A:C4
Cambrian coast line

As can be seen, looking west in the direction of Porthmadog, the station stands on quite a severe curve. Constructed by the Cambrian Railways and opened in 1872, there is an exchange link with the Ffestiniog Railway close by. *12.4.1994*

MORFA MAWDDACH
A:D5

Cambrian coast line

The modern platform is seen here looking north towards Barmouth. Originally opened as a temporary terminus in 1867 and known as 'Barmouth Junction', it took the existing name in 1960.

The second photograph shows the old platform for trains to Dolgellau and beyond when the station was a junction; the Dolgellau line closed in 1965. The modern platform is on the right, looking south towards Fairbourne. *27.5.1994*

MOUNTAIN ASH (Aberpennar)   C:B2
Aberdare branch

The first photograph is a long-distance view of the station, looking south towards Penrhiwceiber, with the Afon Cynon on the left.

The second view provides a close-up of the station, also looking south. This new station was opened on 3 October 1988 with investment capital from Mid Glamorgan CC. *8.6.1995*

NARBERTH (Arberth) B:C4
Pembroke Dock branch
The view along the platform is looking east towards Whitland. The station was opened in 1866 by the Pembroke & Tenby Railway, and the station building is in use by a joinery firm. *28.6.1994*

NEATH (Castell-Nedd) B:F5
South Wales main line
The first station opened in 1850 but in 1864 was replaced by a second one, which itself was replaced by a third in 1877! Known then as 'Neath General', it was re-named by BR to its present title in 1968. The original buildings were demolished and the revamped station opened in 1978. The first picture is the view looking east, and the second shows the new entrance and buildings on the up side. *9.5.1995*

NEWPORT (Casnewydd)
B:H6
South Wales main line
The first picture shows the station looking east towards Severn Tunnel Junction. Most passenger trains use the 'island' platform on the left-hand side of the photograph, while freight traffic mainly uses the two 'through' lines between the platforms to the right. The station was originally opened as 'Newport High Street' in 1850, and was re-named by BR to 'Newport'.

The second picture was taken from the east end of Platform 1, looking west towards Cardiff, while the third shows the forecourt and modernised entrance to the station, situated on the down side. *8.8.1994/3.10.1995/ 21.3.1995*

NEWTOWN (Y Drenewydd)
A:F6

Shrewsbury-Aberystwyth line
The first station was opened by the Llanidloes & Newtown Railway in 1859, but was replaced by the current one in 1861, situated approximately half a mile to the west. It was re-named 'Newtown (Powys)' for a period by BR but ultimately lost the county suffix. The station is a passing place, as seen here looking east towards Welshpool from the down platform.

The second picture shows the main station buildings, situated on the up side. *11.4.1995*

NINIAN PARK (Parc Ninian)
C:D5/6

Cardiff Central-Radyr (City Line)
The view below looking north-west towards Waun-gron Park reveals the simple platforms with waiting shelters. The station dates back to 1912, as an excursion platform, which no doubt followed the opening of Cardiff City's ground in 1910. Known previously as 'Ninian Park Platform' and 'Ninian Park Halt', the station has opened and closed more than once, but the current modernised platforms opened in October 1987, with financial assistance from South Glamorgan CC and grants from ERDF and PRNI. *12.4.1995*

NORTH LLANRWST
(Gogledd Llanrwst)   A:D3
Blaenau Ffestiniog branch
The first station opened in 1863, replaced by the existing one in 1868. It became 'Llanrwst & Trefriw' in 1884, but when a new station was opened nearer the town centre in 1989 as 'Llanrwst', it took the current name. The first view is from the nearby road bridge and shows the station looking north towards Dolgarrog; it is a crossing place, with the only signal box on the branch. The second view is looking south towards Llanrwst.
5.3.1994/29.3.1996

PANTYFFYNNON   B:E4
Central Wales line
The remaining platform is seen here looking south towards Pontarddulais. The station was first mentioned by Bradshaw in June 1857, and the building was designed by I. K. Brunel. The signal box is the only one open south of Craven Arms on the Central Wales line. *25.5.1995*

At Pantyffynnon we are now looking north towards Ammanford from the south end of the platform. On the left is the Central Wales line, and on the right is the freight-only line to Gwaun-cae-Gurwen, which was until 1958 a passenger line to Brynamman. The silo contains sand for locomotives, to assist wheel grip in wet or icy weather. *25.5.1995*

PEMBREY & BURRY PORT (Penbre a Porth Tywyn)　**B:D5**
Swansea-Carmarthen line
This view of the station is looking west towards Kidwelly. Originally opened in 1852 simply as 'Pembrey', it took the existing name in 1887. *25.5.1995*

PEMBROKE (Penfro)　**B:B5**
Pembroke Dock branch
The refurbished platform and waiting shelter are seen in this view looking north-west towards Pembroke Dock. The station was opened in 1863 by the Pembroke & Tenby Railway. *27.6.1994*

PEMBROKE DOCK (Doc Penfro)   **B:B5**
Terminus of branch from Whitland
Opened in 1864 by the Pembroke & Tenby Railway, the station was extensively renovated in 1980 and is a Grade II Listed Building. The first view is towards the buffers and the second from the buffers looking towards Pembroke; only the platform on the right is in use. *27.6.1994*

PENALLY (Penalun)   B:C5
Pembroke Dock branch

The long platform is seen in this view looking towards Tenby. The station has a history of opening and closing. Opened in 1863, it remained so for more than 100 years until closure in 1964; it re-opened in 1970, only to be closed again in November of the same year. Similarly, it opened again in 1971 only to close in the September, finally re-opening in February 1972. Lengthening of the platform was completed by 14 March 1906. The station was used by troops arriving for military exercises in South Pembrokeshire. *29.6.1994*

PENARTH   C:D6
Terminus of branch from Cogan Junction on Cardiff Central-Barry line

Opened in 1878 by the Penarth Harbour, Dock & Railway as 'Penarth Town', the name was revised by BR to simply 'Penarth'. The station was refurbished in 1987, as can be seen from this view looking towards the end of the line, with investment from South Glamorgan CC together with grants from ERDF and PRNI, in co-operation with Regional Railways. *21.9.1994*

PENCOED   B:G6
South Wales main line
The first station here was opened in
1850, and closed in 1964. The new
one opened in May 1992, with
capital investment from Mid
Glamorgan CC. The first picture is
the view looking west towards
Bridgend, taken from the up
platform and showing how far it is
staggered from the down one. The
second picture shows the up platform
and was taken from the footbridge,
looking east towards Pontyclun.
28.6.1995

PENGAM   C:D3
Rhymney Valley line
We are looking north towards
Gilfach Fargoed. Originally opened
in 1858, the station became 'Pengam
& Fleur-de-Lis' in 1909 before
reverting to the present title in 1924,
then '(Glam)' was added as a suffix
until 1968. *27.7.1995*

PENHELIG (Penhelyg)

A:D6

Cambrian coast line
This view of the station is looking
west towards Aberdovey. Opened by
the GWR in 1933 as 'Penhelig Halt',
it was re-named by BR in 1968.
2.3.1994

PENMAENMAWR   A:D2

North Wales coast line
In this view, taken from the station
footbridge looking east towards
Conwy, the entrance to the stone
loading sidings is on the left-hand
side, beyond the signal box. Opened
by the Chester & Holyhead Railway
in 1849 as 'Penmaenmaur' at a cost
of £500, the name was changed to
the present spelling at a later date.
The station underwent various
additions, including the buildings on
the down side, in 1868. A 'bus'-type
shelter was added to the up platform
in 1970. *17.8.1995*

Although the down-side buildings,
seen here from the station approach
road, are in the style of Francis
Thompson, they were not designed
by him. Part is in use by an antiques
firm. *17.8.1995*

PENRHIWCEIBER   C:C3

Aberdare branch

The original station here was opened in 1883, re-named 'Penrhiwceiber Low Level' in 1924, closed in 1964, then refurbished and re-opened in 1988 with the present name, with capital investment by Mid Glamorgan CC. The view is looking north towards Mountain Ash. *8.6.1995*

PENRHYNDEUDRAETH

A:D4

Cambrian coast line

The station, seen here looking west towards Minffordd, was originally opened by the Aberystwyth & Welsh Coast Railway in 1867. *12.4.1994*

PENSARN   A:C4

Cambrian coast line

The view is looking north towards Llandanwg. The original station dated back to its opening in 1867 by the Aberystwyth & Welsh Coast Railway. At one time it became 'Llanbedr & Pensarn' but later reverted to the present name. *12.4.1994*

PENTRE-BACH   C:B/C1
Merthyr Tydfil branch
Comprising a simple platform and waiting shelter, the station is seen looking
north towards Merthyr Tydfil. Opened by the Taff Vale Railway in 1886 as
'Pentrebach', it received the current slightly different form (with hyphen) in
1980. *8.6.1995*

PEN-Y-BONT   B:G2
Central Wales line
Looking north-east towards Dolau, the old down-side platform can be seen on
the right. Opened in 1865 as 'Crossgates', it was re-named 'Penybont' and
finally 'Pen-y-Bont' in 1980. The inset shows a rather old station name sign.
12.8.1994

PENYFFORDD
(Pen-y-ffordd)   A:G3
Bidston-Wrexham Central line
Looking north towards Buckley, beyond the signal box on the left-hand side is the access to the closed branch to Mold. Opened in 1866 by the Wrexham, Mold & Connah's Quay Railway as 'Hope Junction', it was re-named 'Pen-y-Ffordd' or 'Penyffordd', finally settling as the latter. *26.10.1995*

PONTARDDULAIS   B:E5
Central Wales line
At one time the station had four platform faces. It has a long history, dating back to 1850 when opened by the Llanelly Railway as 'Pontardulais'. In 1886 it became a joint GWR/LNWR station. The word 'Halt' was added to the name in 1965, before it received the current name in 1969. This view is looking north towards Pantyffynnon. *25.5.1995*

PONTLOTTYN (Pontlotyn)
C:C1
Rhymney branch
We are looking north towards Rhymney. The station was originally opened in about 1859 by the Rhymney Railway. *27.7.1995*

PONTYCLUN   B:G6

South Wales main line
Looking west from the road bridge,
overlooking the station, the view is
towards Pencoed. This new station
was opened in September 1992 with
financial assistance from Mid
Glamorgan CC. *3.8.1995*

PONT-Y-PANT   A:D3

Blaenau Ffestiniog branch
Opened in 1879, the station lies on a
curve, as can be seen from this view
looking north-east towards Betws-y-
Coed. The second picture provides a
close-up of the station building on
what was the down-side; it is now a
private house. *5.3.1994*

PONTYPOOL & NEW INN (Pont-y-Pwl & New Inn)   B:H5
Hereford-Newport line

The station consists of a wide 'island' platform with a modern waiting shelter. The first view is looking north towards Abergavenny. The first station appeared here in 1854, with the present station opening in 1909, variously known as 'Newport Road', 'Pontypool Road' and 'Pontypool' before reaching the current name in 1994, following refurbishment and official re-opening in May of that year, at a reported cost of £150,000. The 'island' platform originally had a bay at each end. *28.6.1995*

This is the modernised forecourt and station entrance on the east side of the line. The funding came from Gwent CC, Torfaen Borough Council, the Welsh Development Agency, the European Regional Development Fund, BR Community Trust and Regional Railways South Wales & West! *28.6.1995*

PONTYPRIDD   C:C4
Treherbert line

This is where the line from Cardiff splits to Treherbert and Merthyr Tydfil/Aberdare; it remains a large station, but with only two platforms in use. The first picture shows the southbound (Cardiff) platform. In the centre background can be seen a modern platform, which was opened in September 1991 and is used for all northbound services. The station dates back to 1840 as 'Newbridge Junction', becoming 'Pontypridd' in 1866; it then had 'Central' added in 1924 before reverting to the existing name in 1930. *2.9.1994*

The Cardiff platform can be seen again on the left of this view from the footbridge, which connects the old part of the station with the new platform. We are looking south towards Treforest. *2.9.1994*

PORT TALBOT PARKWAY   B:F6
South Wales main line
This view is looking north-west towards Baglan. Comprising an 'island' platform, the station was known as 'Port Talbot' in 1850, became 'Port Talbot & Aberavon' in 1897, then 'Port Talbot General' in 1924, before assuming the current title in 1984. In small letters on the then current (October 1995) station board was added 'For Aberavon Beach'. *9.5.1995*

PORTH   C:B3
Treherbert line
The station is seen here looking north-west towards Dinas Rhondda. At one time the Cardiff platform was an 'island', as can be seen on the right-hand side of the picture. The first station opened in 1861, but was replaced by the current one in 1876, moved a few hundred yards away. *26.4.1995*

PORTHMADOG A:C4

Cambrian coast line

We are looking west towards Criccieth from the road crossing. The station was opened in 1867 as 'Portmadoc'/'Port Madoc', and was re-named to the existing title by BR in 1975. It is a crossing place. *12.4.1994*

PRESTATYN A:F2

North Wales coast line

The first view is looking west along the down platform in the direction of Rhyl. The first station opened here in 1848 but was re-sited and replaced by the current one in 1897. Extended to four platforms in 1899, it has been reduced to the existing 'island' in more recent times.

The second picture shows the 'island' platform looking east towards Flint. The two closed platforms on either side remain in situ. *17.8.1995/16.7.1995*

PWLLHELI   A:B4

Terminus of Cambrian coast line

The single platform is seen looking towards the buffers. On the left is the DMU stabling point, which has basic maintenance facilities. The existing station opened in 1909, having replaced the previous one that dated back to 1867, and was 865 metres to the east. At one time it was described in some timetables as 'Pwllheli for Nevin'. The second picture shows the station frontage following improvements to the road layout. *22.9.1995/29.3.1996*

PYLE (Y Pîl) B:F6
South Wales main line
The basic platforms are seen here looking east towards Bridgend, with modern waiting shelters at the far end. There have been several stations here dating back to 1850. The current station opened in June 1994 with investment by Mid and West Glamorgan CCs. *9.5.1995*

QUAKER'S YARD
(Mynwent y Crynwyr) C:C3
Merthyr Tydfil branch
The station dates back to its opening in 1858; re-named 'Quaker's Yard Low Level' in 1924, BR returned it to its existing name in 1968. The first picture is looking north towards Merthyr Vale, and the second looking south towards Abercynon South. *3.8.1995*

RADYR   C:C5
Cardiff-Pontypridd line
We are looking from the station footbridge south towards Llandaf, with the signal box concealed behind the central signal gantry. The station opened in 1883 as 'Penarth Junction' but was subsequently changed to its current name. *2.9.1994*

This view is also looking south from near the north end of the up platform. The footbridge to the right connects the station with the car park. *2.9.1994*

RHIWBINA   C:D5
Coryton branch
Seen looking west towards Whitchurch, the station consists of a single platform with waiting shelter. In 1987 it underwent refurbishment with financial assistance from South Glamorgan CC and grants from ERDF and PRNI. Originally opened in March 1911 as 'Rhiwbina Platform', then 'Halt', it was given its present title in May 1969. *6.10.1994*

RHOSNEIGR A:B2
North Wales coast line (Anglesey)
Opened originally in 1907 by the LNWR, the station closed in 1917 but re-opened two years later. The wooden buildings were replaced by the more modern ones in the early 1950s. This view is looking north-west towards Valley. *22.6.1993*

RHYL A:E2
North Wales coast line
The first photograph was taken from the down platform looking west towards Abergele. As can be seen, the tracks have been rationalised, with only the two platform lines and one down through road remaining. The station opened in 1848 but had evolved into a larger facility by the early 1900s. *16.7.1993*

The station underwent considerable renovation during 1994/5. The buildings, designed by Francis Thompson, are on a rather grand scale reflecting a much busier railway era. This view is looking west on the up side. *13.10.1995*

RHYMNEY (Rhymni)   C:C1
Terminus of Rhymney Valley line from Cardiff Queen Street
Opened in 1858, the station has undergone modification and has been renovated in relatively recent times. The first picture is from the north end looking south towards Pontlottyn, while the second shows the refurbished station building and forecourt. *27.7.1995*

ROMAN BRIDGE (Y Bont Rufeinig)   **A:D3**
Blaenau Ffestiniog branch
The single platform and station buildings (in private use) are seen looking south-west towards Blaenau Ffestiniog. Opened in 1879, at one time the station name had a 'Halt' suffix. *5.3.1994*

RUABON (Rhiwabon)   **A:G4**
Chester-Shrewsbury line
As seen from the down platform, looking north towards Wrexham General, at one time the station had an 'island' platform, with the footbridge continuing to the left across the now lifted tracks. Opened by the Shrewsbury & Chester Railway in 1846, the station has seen much busier times. *20.8.1993*

SARN   B:F6
Maesteg branch
This new station, seen here looking north towards Tondu, opened in September 1992 with capital investment by Mid Glamorgan CC. *28.6.1995*

SAUNDERSFOOT   B:C5
Pembroke Dock branch
The remaining platform is seen looking north towards Kilgetty. The station was opened in 1866 by the Pembroke & Tenby Railway but was re-sited in 1868. It was subsequently reduced to a single platform. *29.6.1994*

SEVERN TUNNEL JUNCTION (Cyffordd Twnel Hafren) B:I6
South Wales main line

This large station was opened in 1886, though today it is unmanned, with modern waiting shelters and a very long footbridge. The first picture is looking west towards Newport.

The second view is from below the station footbridge, also looking west towards Newport. Considerable track simplification has taken place. There was a loco depot nearby, which closed in 1987. *21.3.1995*

SHOTTON HIGH LEVEL
A:G2/3

Bidston-Wrexham Central line

This view is looking north-east towards Hawarden Bridge. The stations at Shotton, on two levels, are connected by a footpath, and the entrance and station buildings are situated at the High Level facility. Opened originally as 'Connah's Quay & Shotton' by the Wrexham, Mold & Connah's Quay Railway in 1891, it was re-named 'Shotton High Level' in 1953 before amalgamated by BR with the low-level station as 'Shotton'. *7.3.1996*

SHOTTON LOW LEVEL
A:G2
North Wales coast line
Seen here looking north towards
Flint, the station was opened by the
LNWR in 1907 as 'Shotton'. It
closed in 1966, but re-opened in
1972 and was re-named 'Shotton
Low Level' shortly afterwards.
Subsequently both levels were
referred to simply as 'Shotton'.
19.7.1994

SKEWEN (Sgiwen)   **B:F5**
South Wales main line
This long-distance view of the station
is looking east towards Neath. The
first station here opened in 1882 as
'Dynevor', and was re-named to the
present title in 1904 before closure in
1910. A second re-sited station lasted
until 1964, but then a modernised
and also re-sited version opened in
June 1994. *9.5.1995*

SUGAR LOAF   **B:F3**
Central Wales line
Perhaps the most basic station in
Wales, Sugar Loaf is seen here
looking north-east towards
Llanwrtyd. It was originally opened
in 1899 as a Staff Halt, used by
railway personnel working on the
nearby tunnel or employed to pin
down brakes on heavy freights.
Known as 'Sugar Loaf Summit',
being 820 feet above sea level, it has
been closed and re-opened three
times since 1949. The platform was
re-named to the present title and re-
opened by BR in 1989. A 'request
stop', it is used mainly by hikers in
the summer months for occasional
use, then in 1992 it appeared in the
public timetable, and on a regular
basis from 1995. *20.5.1995*

SWANSEA (Abertawe)

B:E5

Terminus of South Wales main line
At Swansea down passenger trains
going further west have to reverse,
similarly trains from the west going
east. Opened in 1850, at one time as
'Swansea High Street', it was
originally broad gauge, converted to
standard in 1872. It was rebuilt in
1934 by the GWR, and subsequently
modernised by BR in the 1980s,
being given its present title in 1968.

The first picture is looking towards
the buffers, and the second shows the
west-side platforms looking north.
The impressive outside of the station,
faced with ashlar stone, is seen in the
third photograph. *9.5.1995 (2)/
4.4.1996*

TAFFS WELL (Fynnon Taf)   C:C4
Cardiff-Pontypridd line
The station opened in 1863 as Walnut Tree Junction, taking its present name in 1900. This view is looking north from the station footbridge towards Treforest Estate. The second picture shows the modern station building on the west (up) side of the line. *3.8.1995*

TALSARNAU   A:D4
Cambrian coast line
The station was opened in 1867 by the Aberystwyth & Welsh Coast Railway, at one time with a hyphen as 'Tal-Sarnau'. We are looking north towards Llandecwyn. *12.4.1994*

TALYBONT   A:C5
Cambrian coast line
This view of the modernised platform and waiting shelter is looking north towards Dyffryn Ardudwy. The first station here was opened in 1914 by the Cambrian Railways as 'Talybont Halt', and BR gave it its current name in 1968. *12.4.1994*

TAL-Y-CAFN (Talycafn)   **A:E2**
Blaenau Ffestiniog branch
The station buildings are seen here from the level crossing, looking north towards Glan Conwy. Opened originally in 1863 by the Conway & Llanrwst Railway, the station was later re-named 'Tal-y-Cafn & Eglwysbach', but subsequently reverted to the original name. *5.3.1994*

Another view of the station buildings, situated on what was the down platform, looking south towards Dolgarrog. The five-lever ground frame for the crossing can be seen on the platform behind the 'Stop' sign. *5.3.1994*

TENBY (Dinbych-y-pysgod)
B:C5
Pembroke Dock branch
The station opened in 1866, replacing the original Pembroke & Tenby Railway station, which had been opened in 1863 and closed three years later. The station is a crossing place, and is seen here looking north towards Saundersfoot.

The second picture shows the station forecourt and refurbished entrance on the east side of the line. *29.6.1994*

TIR-PHIL   C:D2
Rhymney branch
Opened in March 1858, at one time the station was known as 'Tir Phil & New Tredegar' and other variations until finally the current name was adopted in 1980. We are looking south towards Brithdir. *27.7.1995*

TONDU   B:F6
Maesteg branch
The modern platform and waiting shelter are seen looking north towards Garth. Tondu is the junction with the freight-only line from Margam to Blaengarw, which leaves the Maesteg line north of the station. The station here dates back to 1864, but it closed in 1970. The existing new station was opened in September 1992, with financial investment from Mid Glamorgan CC. *28.6.1995*

TONFANAU   A:C6
Cambrian coast line
The platform and waiting shelter are seen looking south towards the road crossing and Tywyn. The station opened in 1896 'solely for the use of one or two local residents – not to be advertised'! Apparently closed for a short period from about 1897 to 1902, in 1994 BR made application to close it, and in the Winter timetable of 1995/6 it was noted that it might close during the lifetime of the timetable, but it was reprieved by the Department of Transport on the grounds of likely damage to the tourist trade and hardship to local residents, so it remains open. The second view shows the waiting shelter from the road crossing, looking north towards Llwyngwril. *27.5.1995*

TON PENTRE   C:A3
Treherbert line
The refurbished platform and shelter are seen here looking north-west towards Treorchy. Originally opened in 1861 as 'Ystrad', it became 'Y Rhondda' before gaining its present name in 1986. *26.4.1995*

TONYPANDY   C:B3
Treherbert line
The station opened in 1908 as 'Tonypandy & Trealaw', which it remained until 1973 when it was simplified to the present title. The long platform is seen in the first picture looking south towards Dinas Rhondda, and in the second picture looking north towards Llwynypia. As can be seen, the station is conveniently situated for the local Bingo Hall! *26.4.1995*

TREFOREST (Trefforest)   C:C4
Cardiff-Pontypridd line
This is the station looking north towards Pontypridd. The first station opened in 1846 as 'Treforest' and was re-named 'Treforest Low Level' in 1924 before receiving the existing title in 1980. *2.9.1994*

TREFOREST ESTATE (Ystrad Trefforest)   C:C4
Cardiff-Pontypridd line
Looking south towards Taffs Well, the station consists of an 'island' platform with a modest waiting shelter. It was opened during the Second World War (in 1942), possibly as a workmen's rather than a public station. *3.8.1995*

TREHAFOD C:C3
Treherbert line
The station, seen here looking west towards Porth, replaced nearby Hafod, which had opened in 1861, taking the present title in 1905. To the left is part of the Rhondda Heritage Park at the former Lewis Merthyr Colliery. *26.4.1995*

TREHERBERT C:A3
Terminus of line from Radyr and Pontypridd
The refurbished station is seen looking towards the end of the line, with sidings on the left. The station was opened in 1863 by the Taff Vale Railway. *26.4.1995*

TREORCHY (Treorci)
C:A3
Treherbert line
This is another refurbished station, and the view is looking north towards Ynyswen. The first station had opened in 1869 as 'Treorky', and was replaced by the existing one in 1884, becoming 'Treorchy' around the turn of the 20th century. *26.4.1995*

TROED-Y-RHIW C:C2
Merthyr Tydfil branch
We are looking north towards Pentre-bach, and the disused southbound platform can be seen on the right. The station opened in 1841 as 'Troedyrhiew' but changed to the current name in 1980. *3.8.1995*

TY CROES A:B2
North Wales coast line (Anglesey)
The station was opened by the Chester & Holyhead Railway in 1848. Looking north towards Rhosneigr, the first picture shows the down platform, and the second the up platform looking east towards Bodorgan. *22.6.1993*

TY GLAS   C:D5
Coryton branch
Seen looking west towards Birchgrove, this new station was opened on 29 April 1987 with financial support from South Glamorgan CC and Regional Railways, and with the help of ERDF and PRNI grants. *6.10.1994*

TYGWYN   A:C4
Cambrian coast line
The single platform is seen looking north towards Talsarnau. Opened by the GWR in 1927, it was then known as 'Tygwyn Halt', but lost the word 'Halt' in 1968. Application by BR in 1994 to close the station was refused by the Department of Transport following a public inquiry. *12.4.1994*

TYWYN   A:C6
Cambrian coast line
The first picture shows both platforms, looking south towards Aberdovey. Opened in 1863 by the Aberystwyth & Welsh Coast Railway as 'Towyn', the name was changed to the different spelling by BR in 1975. The second picture provides a closer look at the station buildings situated on the up platform. *27.5.1994*

VALLEY (Y Dyffryn) A:B2
North Wales coast line (Anglesey)
Viewed here from the road crossing, looking north-west towards Holyhead, Valley station was opened in 1849 by the
Chester & Holyhead Railway; the station building was designed by Francis Thompson. The station closed in 1966 but
re-opened in March 1982. *22.6.1993*

WAUN-GRON PARK (Parc Waun-gron) C:D5
Cardiff Central-Radyr (City Line)
This new station opened in November 1987 with capital investment by South Glamorgan CC and grants from ERDF
and PRNI in co-operation with Regional Railways. Looking north towards Fairwater, it can be seen that the platforms
are partly staggered. *12.4.1995*

WELSHPOOL (Y Trallwng)
A:F5
Shrewsbury-Aberystwyth line
Viewed from the station approach footbridge, looking north-east towards Shrewsbury, the modern station consists of an 'island' platform. The original station here was opened in 1860 by the Oswestry & Newtown Railway, later absorbed by the Cambrian. When the town bypass was built, the old station was closed and a new one constructed close by on a re-aligned line, opening in May 1992. *20.8.1993*

Looking from the nearby road bridge during construction of the new bypass, the original station building (built as the headquarters of the Oswestry & Newtown Railway) is on the left. It is in the 'French Renaissance' style and by the end of 1995 was being renovated for alternative use as a joint venture between the Development Board for Rural Wales and Montgomeryshire District Council. *5.2.1993*

Looking at the other side of this remarkable building during renovation, its size can be seen. A ceremony took place in the spring of 1996 marking the completion of the restoration, and the building will be used by Edinburgh Woollen Mills as a retail outlet/tourist attraction. *19.10.1995*

WHITCHURCH (Yr Eglwys Newydd) C:D5
Coryton branch
This view is eastwards towards Rhiwbina. The original station opened in 1911, subsequently becoming 'Whitchurch (Glam.)' in 1924, then 'Whitchurch (South Glam)' in 1975 before reverting to the present name. It was refurbished in 1987 with financial support from South Glamorgan CC and grants from ERDF and PRNI, in co-operation with Regional Railways. *6.10.1994*

WHITLAND (Hendy-gwyn) B:C4
Carmarthen-Fishguard Harbour line
We are looking west towards Clunderwen, and the Pembroke Dock branch leaves the main line here just beyond the platforms, curving away to the south-west. The station dates back to 1854, when there was just a single broad-gauge track. In the late 1860s the junction was formed with the Pembroke & Tenby Railway. The station has been refurbished and given a new entrance. *29.6.1994*

WILDMILL (Melin Wyllt)
B:F6
Maesteg branch
This new station, seen here looking south towards Bridgend, was built with capital assistance from Mid Glamorgan CC, and opened towards the end of 1992. *28.6.1995*

WREXHAM CENTRAL (Wrecsam Canolog)   A:G3
Terminus of line from Bidston

The station opened in 1887 following extension of the line from the previous 'Central' station, which was re-named 'Exchange'. In 1895 the station ceased to be a terminus following the construction of the line to Ellesmere, necessitating the building of new platforms and footbridge. The Cambrian Railways (ultimately part of the GWR) worked the Ellesmere line and by 1901 the Great Central (later a constituent of the LNER) had control of the Bidston line, so Central saw a variety of stock and locomotives. In September 1962 passenger services ended on the Ellesmere line, so Central reverted to being a terminal station. In 1998 the station was re-sited to allow for a retail development, and presently consists of a single platform and waiting shelter, as seen in the first view, looking from the buffer stop towards Wrexham General.

The full length of the remaining platform, looking towards the buffers, can be seen in the second picture. Before closure the Ellesmere line continued to the right of the church. *10.6.1994*

WREXHAM GENERAL (Wrecsam Cyffredinol)   **A:G3**
Chester-Shrewsbury line

Looking north towards Chester, the track on the left is the connection between the main line and the Wrexham Central to Bidston line, and the platforms are connected by the footbridge on the left. The original station was opened in 1846 by the Shrewsbury & Chester Railway, and was rebuilt in 1875 by the GWR. A £300,000 refurbishment programme was approved in 1995, and the station has Grade II Listed status.

   The second photograph shows the view from the road bridge looking south towards Ruabon. In the far distance is Croes Newydd North Fork signal box and a busy road crossing. *20.8.1993*

The main Wrexham General station buildings on the up side are built in the 'French Pavilion' style with decorative iron railings. *20.8.1993*

This is the platform on the Wrexham Central to Bidston line, looking north towards Gwersyllt. When the extension towards the town centre was opened, the new terminus was called 'Central', and this part of the station became 'Exchange' until it was finally amalgamated under the 'General' name in 1981, and a new footbridge connected the two parts of the station. *20.8.1993*

YNYSWEN   C:A3
Treherbert line
This new station, seen here looking
north towards Treherbert, opened in
September 1986 with capital
investment from Mid Glamorgan
CC. *26.4.1995*

YSTRAD MYNACH   C:D3
Rhymney Valley line
As can be seen in this view looking
north towards Hengoed, the
platforms are staggered. The original
station opened in 1858 as 'Ystrad',
and was re-named to the present title
in 1891. *27.7.1995*

YSTRAD RHONDDA
C:A3
Treherbert line
A new station, it opened in
September 1986 with capital
investment from Mid Glamorgan
CC. The station is a crossing place
and is seen here looking south-east
towards Llwynypia. *26.4.1995*

New stations and major alterations since privatisation

In addition to the following, new stations are to be opened during 2007/8 between Newport and Ebbw Vale at ROGERSTONE, RISCA, CROSS KEYS, NEWBRIDGE (EBBW VALE), LLANHILLETH and EBBW VALE (PARKWAY). In December 2007 a new station opened at LLANHARAN (between Pontyclun and Pencoed).

BARRY DOCKS (Dociau'r Barri)   C:C7
Cardiff Central-Barry Island line
A new overall canopy is being constructed and expected to be opened before the end of 2007. (See also page 53)
11.9.2007

CARDIFF CENTRAL (Caerdydd Canolog)   C:D5
South Wales main line
A new platform is being added on the up (north) side of the line, to be known as Platform 0. This is the view looking east with a Central Trains Class 170 forming a service to Nottingham. (See also pages 63-4) *21.8.2007*

LLANTWIT MAJOR (Llanilltud Fawr)   B:G6

Former freight-only Barry-Bridgend line

The first station opened in 1897 and closed in 1964. This new one opened on 12 June 2005 and is seen here looking west towards Bridgend. The bay at the east end of the latter station was re-instated as a dedicated platform for the services from Cardiff via the Vale of Glamorgan line.

The second picture shows the main entrance to the station on the down side. It is an interchange with local bus services. *15.5.2007*

NEWPORT (Casnewydd)   B:H6
South Wales main line
The disused platform on the up side, north-west of the line (see page 116), has been fully refurbished and is seen here looking east. This 'new' platform, No 4, will greatly relieve the shortage of platforms. It is 273 yards long and was made available for use on 2 July 2007, and officially opened five days later. *21.8.2007*

This is the view overlooking the closed Godfrey Road stabling point, with the new platform on the right. *15.5.2007*

RHOOSE CARDIFF INTERNATIONAL AIRPORT (Y Rhws Maes Awyr Rhyngwladol Caerdydd)   B:G7
Former freight-only Barry-Bridgend line
The first view is looking west along the up platform with the down platform beyond the road crossing. This new station opened on 12 June 2005, primarily to cater for air travellers using Cardiff Airport; there is a regular bus service from the station to the airport.

The second picture is looking towards Barry along the up platform with the rear of Class 143 No 143601 departing eastbound. *15.5.2007*

WREXHAM CENTRAL
(Wrecsam Canolog)   A:G3
Terminus of line from Bidston
This new station opened in
November 1998, following the
closure of the old station (see page
156) to allow for a large shopping
area development. Built 400 yards
closer to General station, as can be
seen it has a modern entrance and
waiting area between the shops.
27.10.1999

The new station is seen here from the
nearby road bridge, showing the
single platform. In the distance is the
Parish Church of St Giles, which is
close to the position of the old
station. *27.10.1999*

MACHYNLLETH   A:D6
Shrewsbury-Aberystwyth line
Arriva Trains Wales opened a new
depot in 2007 where the company's
fleet of Class 158 DMUs will be
maintained. *13.8.2007; photo
courtesy of Arriva Trains Wales*

Signalling in Wales, 1995

At the end of 1995 there were more than 60 signal boxes open in Wales. These varied from the smallest non-block post controlling a level crossing, such as Llanfair PG on Anglesey, to the power box covering a wide area around Cardiff. They can be divided into various categories. First are the oldest mechanical boxes, a number of which dated back to the 19th century, including Ty Croes (1872) in the north, Caersws (1891) in mid-Wales and Ystrad Mynach (1886) in South Wales. Most of these boxes operated some semaphore signals – upper-quadrants dominating in North Wales and lower-quadrants in South Wales, with some exceptions. Next are the boxes controlling colour lights such as Bangor and Kidwelly. The third category is the larger power boxes such as Cardiff and Newport, usually covering a considerable area. Finally there is the most modern installation, RETB (Radio Electronic Token Block), with just one example in Wales, operating on the Cambrian line from a central control at Machynlleth; communication is made directly between signalman and train driver and electronic 'tokens' passed by radio link. A system known as NSKT (No Signalman Key Token) is used on a number of single lines, such as Craven Arms to Pantyffynnon. At passing loops on such lines the trailing points are hydro-pneumatically operated by the train wheels and drivers use lineside telephones/instruments connected to the controlling signal box for permission to proceed. Both RETB and NSKT have been vital to the economical working – and survival – of such rural lines by enabling most signal boxes to be dispensed with.

Signal boxes that were closed but remained in situ at the end of 1995 included BARMOUTH SOUTH (a listed building), CEFN JUNCTION (Ogmore Vale Extension, in use as a Field Study Centre), COLWYN BAY, LLANDEILO (demolished in March 1996), LLANUWCHLLYN (in use by the Bala Lake Railway), PENMAENPOOL (Information Centre/RSPB), RHYL No 2 (a listed building), and BRYN-Y-GWYNON CROSSING. Two other boxes designated as listed buildings within the Principality are LLANDRINDOD WELLS (listed, and in use as a Museum) and LLANGOLLEN STATION on the Llangollen Railway.

Abbreviations

GF	Ground Frame
NSKT	No Signalman Key Token
NSTR	No Signalman Key Token Remotely Controlled
PSB	Power signal box
RETB	Radio Electronic Token Block
CB	Crossing Box
GB	Gate Box
LC	Level crossing
P	'Portakabin'-type box

A-Z of signal boxes open at the end of 1995

The following signal boxes, crossing boxes and ground frames (those with a building) were open as at 31 December 1995. The letters in brackets after the box name are the box code. The date of opening refers to the box illustrated – there may have been earlier boxes on the site.

ABERBEEG JUNCTION (AB)
Ebbw Vale freight-only line
Of a GWR design dating from 1892. Closed 14 December 1997. *13.6.1996*

ABERCYNON (A/AB)   C:C3
Merthyr Tydfil branch
The box is situated at the Cardiff end of the platform of Abercynon South station.
A GWR design, the box opened in 1932, having originally been at Birmingham Moor Street (1909), then Didcot Foxhall Junction (1915). *2.9.1994*

ABERGAVENNY (A)   B:H4
Hereford-Newport line
The box is south of the station, on the east side of the line. Of GWR design, it dates back to 1934. *3.8.1995*

ABERGELE (AE)   A:E2
North Wales coast line
An LNWR design dating back to 1902, it is situated between the up and down lines in the middle of the station. It is a Grade II listed building. *19.7.1996*

ABERTHAW (A/AW)
B:G7
Barry-Bridgend freight-only line
A Barry Railway design dating back to 1897, the box controls access to Aberthaw Power Station. *12.9.1996*

BANGOR (BR)   A:C2
North Wales coast line
The box is on the north of the station on the up side. It is an LNWR design dating back to 1923, and was previously Bangor No 2 – No 1 box closed on 8 December 1968. The photo is looking north, and shows the entrance to Belmont Tunnel. *25.3.1994*

BARGOED (B/BD)   C:D2
Rhymney Valley line
The box is north of the station on the east side of the line. It is a replacement box, of WR design, opened on 9 November 1970, having previously been at Cymmer Afan. It is located at the start of the double track heading to Cardiff Queen Street. *27.7.1995*

BARRY (B)   C:C7
Cardiff Central-Barry Island line
This box of Barry Railway design, dating back to around 1897, is at the Cardiff end of the down platform. *6.1.1999*

BARRY ISLAND (BI)   C:C7
Terminus of branch from Barry
The box is at the Barry end of Platform 1, and opened on 5 May 1929 as Barry Island West, of McKenzie & Holland design. (Barry Island East opened the same day, but closed in 1964.) Closed 16 March 1998, and subsequently dismantled. *21.9.1994*

BISHTON CROSSING
South Wales main line, between Newport and Severn Tunnel Junction
Of GWR design, the box opened in February 1941, and has been a gate box since 17 April 1961. Its reduced frame of three levers (plus two for the wicket gates) rates special mention! *5.6.1996*

CAERSWS (CS)   A:E6
Shrewsbury-Aberystwyth line
The box is situated at the east end of the station on the up side, and has been a gate box since 21 October 1988. It is a Dutton (Cambrian) design, and opened in 1891. It is also a Grade II listed building. *13.9.1996*

CALDICOT GF (CA)   B:I6
Gloucester-Newport line
The box is east of Caldicot station on the down side of the line. A hut on a brick base, it is a BR (WR) design and opened in about 1979. As well as being a gate box, it also controls access to the Caerwent and Sudbrook branches. *5.6.1996*

CARDIFF PSB (C/CF) C:D5
South Wales main line
Located by Central station on the
down side, it is a BR (WR) design
and opened in March 1966. *9.5.1995*

CARMARTHEN JUNCTION (CJ) B:D4
South Wales main line
The box is situated off the Swansea-
Fishguard Harbour line, on the east
curve out of the station leading to the
up main line. Of BR (WR) design, it
opened on 5 February 1956.
26.6.1996

CLARBESTON ROAD (CR)
B:B4
Carmarthen-Fishguard Harbour line
The box is opposite the junction for
Haverfordwest and beyond, and
where the double-track main line
becomes single. Of GWR design, it
opened 23 August 1906. *25.6.1996*

COWBRIDGE ROAD (CR)
Barry-Bridgend freight-only line, east of Bridgend
This BR (WR) hut is on the down side of the line, and opened 12 September 1965. *4.4.1996*

CROES NEWYDD NORTH FORK (CN)
Chester-Shrewsbury line, south of Wrexham General station
The box is on the up side. Of GWR design, it opened in 1905 and controls a busy level crossing. *10.6.1994*

DEE MARSH JUNCTION (DM)
Bidston-Wrexham line, north of Hawarden Bridge station
The last remaining working GCR box in Wales, dating back to 1930, it is located on the west side of the line. It controls the entrance to Shotton Steelworks sidings. *19.7.1994*

DEGANWY (DY)   A:D2
Llandudno branch
The box is at the Llandudno end of the station by the down platform. Of LNWR design, it opened in 1914 as Deganwy No 2 (No 1 box closed on 4 June 1967). It controls the nearby road crossing. *30.12.1993*

EAST USK (MU/EU/M)
South Wales main line, east of Newport
The box is located on the down side of the line, by the reception sidings and where the branch line to Uskmouth (Fifoots Point Power Station) heads south. Opened on 16 April 1961 by BR (WR), it controls the sidings and branch, but other lines are under the control of Newport PSB. *13.6.1996*

FERRYSIDE (F/FS)   **B:D4**
Swansea-Carmarthen line
The box is situated at the west end of the down platform. A GWR design, it opened in the 1880s. *25.5.1995*

GAERWEN (GN)
North Wales coast line (Anglesey), west of Llanfair PG
On the up side, the box controlled access to the Amlwch branch (the connection to the branch was subsequently removed and plain-lined). Of LNWR design, it opened in 1882 as Gaerwen No 1 (No 2 boxed closed 11 December 1966). It also controls a level crossing. *16.6.1994*

HEATH JUNCTION (HJ)
C:D5
Rhymney Valley line
This 'Portakabin'-type box is situated on the Cardiff side of Heath High Level station, on the east side of the line. It opened on 20 November 1984. *28.11.1995*

HOLYHEAD (HD)   A:B2
Terminus of North Wales coast line (Anglesey)
Photographed from a passing train, the box is just south of the station on the up side. An LMS design, it opened in 1938 and, with 100 levers, rates as one of the largest boxes in the Principality. *10.11.1993*

HOLYWELL JUNCTION (HJ)
North Wales coast line north-west of Flint, opposite former Holywell Junction station
The box is located between the up and down main lines. An LNWR-style box, it opened in 1902 and is Grade II listed. The ship in the background is the ex-Isle of Man ferry *Duke of Lancaster*, which is beached in concrete. *5.12.1993*

KIDWELLY (K)   B:D5
Swansea-Carmarthen line
The box is situated at the east end of the station on the down side. It consists of a BR (WR) design mounted on a much older GWR brick base (dating back to 1885) in the 1950s. *25.5.1995*

LIME KILN SIDINGS (LK)
Ebbw Vale freight-only line
A GWR design, it opened in 1887 on the west side of the line. It was reduced to gate box status on 14 December 1997, and was subsequently closed and demolished in 2007. *13.6.1996*

LITTLE MILL JUNCTION (LM)
Hereford-Newport line, south of Pontypool & New Inn station
The box is on the east side of the line and is a McKenzie & Holland (GWR) design, opened in 1883. It was once the junction for the line to Ross-on-Wye, then the freight-only line to Glascoed. *13.6.1996*

LLANDAF LOOP JUNCTION (LL) C:D5
Cardiff Queen Street-Radyr line
The box is just north of Llandaf station on east side of the line. A Taff Railway design, it opened in 1900, and controlled the exit from Radyr Yard at north end of Llandaf station. It closed on 12 May 1998, superseded by the new Radyr Junction 'Portakabin' panel box, opened the same day. *12.9.1996*

LLANDARCY GF
Briton Ferry-Central Wales freight-only line, east of Swansea
Situated on the west side of the line, this GWR-design box opened in 1920, and was reduced to a GF on 24 February 1973. Previously known as 'Lon Las South', it controls access to the BP oil refinery. *7.10.1997*

LLANDUDNO (LO)   A:D2
Terminus of branch from Llandudno Junction
The box is situated at the south end of the station on the down side. An LNWR design, it opened in 1891 as Llandudno No 2 (No 1 box closed on 13 September 1970). *17.8.1995*

LLANDUDNO JUNCTION (LJ)   A:D2
North Wales coast line
Situated on the west of the station on the up side, this BR (LMR) design is a relatively modern box, opened on 17 February 1985 and containing an NX panel. For a time it stood side by side with its LNWR 1898 predecessor, Llandudno Junction No 2 (No 1 box closed on 26 May 1968). *17.9.1993*

LLANELLI WEST GF   B:E5
Swansea-Carmarthen line
Standing west of the station on the down side, this was formerly Llanelli No 4 box, of GWR design and dating back to 1877. It was reduced to gate box status on 3 February 1969. *25.5.1995*

LLANFAIR PG   A:C2
North Wales coast line (Anglesey)
The box is on the Bangor side of the station, on the north side of the line. It is an LNWR/C&H-design box dating back to about 1871. It became a gate box on 2 December 1973. *16.6.1994*

LLANRWST & TREFRIW
A:D3
Blaenau Ffestiniog branch
The box is north of North Llanrwst
station on the west side of the line.
Of LNWR design, it opened in 1880
and is now the only signal box on the
branch. *5.3.1994*

LLANTRISANT WEST GF
*South Wales main line, west of
Pontyclun station*
This BR (WR) gate hut is on the up
side of the line, and opened on 5 June
1966. *16.9.1997*

MACHYNLLETH (MH)
A:D6
Shrewsbury-Aberystwyth line
This BR (WR)-style box opened in
1960 east of the station on the up
side. It controls the whole of the line
from Sutton Bridge Junction
(Shrewsbury) to
Aberystwyth/Pwllheli by RETB.
27.5.1994

MAESMAWR
Cardiff-Pontypridd line, between Treforest Estate and Treforest
Photographed from a passing train, the box was on the east side of the line. Of GWR design, it dated back to approximately 1930. It closed on 27 January 1997. *12.4.1995*

MOLD JUNCTION (MJ)
North Wales coast line, between Chester and Shotton
Situated on the down side of the line, this LNWR-design box opened in 1902 and was previously Mold Junction No 1. It closed on 24 January 2005 and was demolished the following month. This photograph was taken from a train. *24.9.1997*

MOSTYN (MN)
North Wales coast line, west of Flint between Holywell Junction and Prestatyn near the site of the former Mostyn station
The box is located between the up and down lines controlling entry to the Exchange and Dock sidings. An LNWR-design box that opened in 1902, it was previously Mostyn No 1 (No 2 box closed in 1942). It is opened as required, and is a Grade II listed building. The Dee estuary can be seen beyond the box. *5.12.1993*

NEATH & BRECON JUNCTION (NB)
North-east of Neath on the Onllwyn and Cwmgwrach (Aberpergwm) freight-only branches
The box, of GWR design, opened in 1892. The South Wales main line crosses on the bridge beyond the signal box. *4.4.1996*

NEWPORT PSB (N)   B:H6
South Wales main line
The box is located at the east end of the station on the down side. It opened in December 1962 and is of BR (WR) design. *8.8.1994*

PANTYFFYNNON SOUTH (PF) B:E4

Central Wales line

This GWR-design box, dating back to 1892, is south of the station on the east side of the line, and is a Grade II listed building. it controls the line to Craven Arms to the north with NSTR, and is also the junction of the freight-only line to Gwaun-cae-Gurwen. 'South' was dropped from the name when Pantyffynnon North box closed on 13 March 1966. *25.5.1995*

PARK JUNCTION (PJ)

Ebbw Vale freight-only line from Ebbw Junction on South Wales main line

The box is on the west side of the line. A McKenzie & Holland/GWR design, it opened in 1885 and, with 100 levers, rates it as one of the largest boxes in Wales. *13.6.1996*

PEMBREY (PY) B:D5

Swansea-Carmarthen line

The box is east of Pembrey & Burry Port station on the north side of the line by the level crossing. It is a GWR design dating back to 1907, and was previously 'Pembrey East', but the suffix was dropped on 4 November 1932 when Pembrey West box closed. *25.5.1995*

PENCOED CROSSING GF
B:G6
South Wales main line
The box was located west of Pencoed station up platform, opposite the down platform. It was a GWR design and opened in about 1905. It had previously been Pencoed East, but the suffix was dropped on 26 October 1964 when Pencoed West box closed. It was reduced to a gate box on 13 September 1965, taken out of use on 31 March 2007 and demolished on 6 April 2007. *8.6.1995*

PENMAENMAWR (PR)
A:D2
North Wales coast line
The box, of BR (LMR) design and dating back to December 1952, is on the down side, east of the station. It controls the stone loading sidings, which are on the up side of the line. *17.8.1995*

PENYFFORDD   A:G3
Bidston-Wrexham Central line
The box is north of the station on the down side. It is a BR (LMR) design dating back to 17 December 1972, and the photo is looking north towards Buckley. *26.10.1995*

PONTYPRIDD JUNCTION (P)   C:C4
Treherbert line, junction with Aberdare branch
The box is north-east of the station, in the fork of the two lines, and is a Taff Vale design dating back to 1902. A Grade II listed building, it closed on 15 October 1998, the area now being controlled by the new Radyr Junction 'Portakabin'-type panel box. *8.6.1995*

PORT TALBOT PSB (PT)   B:F6
South Wales main line
The power box is opposite the station on the down side. A BR (WR) design, it opened on 22 September 1963. *9.5.1995*

PORTH   C:B3
Treherbert line
Opened on 29 March 1981, the box was west of the station on the south side of the line. A BR (WR) design, it supervised NSTR to Treherbert. It closed on 15 October 1998, the area now being controlled by the new Radyr Junction 'Portakabin'-type panel box. *26.4.1995*

PRESTATYN (PN)   A:F2
North Wales coast line
Situated at the west end of the station on the down side of the line, this LNWR-design box opened in 1897. It was formerly Prestatyn No 2 (No 1 box closed on 29 January 1931). The photograph was taken from a train. *17.8.1995*

PWLLHELI WEST FRAME
A:B4
Terminus of Cambrian coast line
Situated at the east end of the station on the south side of the line, this Dutton/Cambrian-design box opened in 1909. It is not a block post, and is open as required. *23.9.1985*

RADYR JUNCTION (VR)   C:C5
Cardiff-Pontypridd line
Situated at the Cardiff end of the station on the east side of the line, this BR (WR)-design box opened on 9 June 1961; the box and frame were from Swindon East (although it was never opened there). Radyr Yard is off to the right. The box closed on 12 May 1998 and was replaced by the new Radyr Junction 'Portakabin'-type panel box, opened the same day. *2.9.1994*

RADYR QUARRY JUNCTION (RQ)
Cardiff Central-Radyr (City Line), between Danescourt and Radyr stations
Located on the west side of the line, this Taff Vale-design box opened in 1899 and closed on 12 May 1998 to be superseded by the new Radyr Junction 'Portakabin'-type panel box, opened the same day. *13.6.1996*

RHYL (RL)   A:E2
North Wales coast line
Standing at the east end of the station on the up side, this Grade II listed LNWR-design box opened in 1900, and was previously known as Rhyl No 1. Rhyl No 2 (closed on 25 March 1990) is also listed and survives at the west end of the station on the up side. *8.1993*

ROCKCLIFFE HALL (RH)
North Wales coast line, between Flint and Shotton Low Level
On the up side of the line, this two-storey 'Portakabin'-type box with a switch panel replaced the previous box on 26 February 1995. The photograph was taken from a train. *13.7.1995*

ST FAGANS GF
South Wales main line, approximately half-way between Pontyclun and Cardiff Central
Located on the up side, this BR (WR) gate box was commissioned in June 1986 when it replaced the previous GF, located opposite. *28.3.1996*

SANDYCROFT (ST)
North Wales coast line, between Chester and Shotton LL
The box was situated between the up and down main lines and is seen here looking north. An LNWR design dating from 1900, it closed on 24 January 2005 and was demolished shortly afterwards. *10.11.1993*

TALACRE (TE)
North Wales coast line, between Prestatyn and Flint, west of Mostyn
Photographed from a passing train, the box is on the north (up) side of the line and is an LNWR design dating back to 1903. It controls the entry into Point of Ayr Colliery sidings. *23.10.1993*

TONDU (TU)   B:F6
Maesteg branch
In this view looking north, the
Maesteg branch is to the left and the
freight-only lines to Pontycymer/
Blaengarw and Caedu to the right.
It is a GWR design dating back to
1884, and was formerly Tondu
Middle. *28.6.1995*

TY CROES (TS)   A:B2
North Wales coast line (Anglesey)
The box is on the up side of the line,
west of the level crossing. An
LNWR/C&H design dating back to
1872, it was downgraded to a gate
box on 2 April 1989. It is now Grade
II listed and contains one of the
smallest frames in Wales, reduced to
six levers. *22.7.1995*

VALLEY (VY)   A:B2
North Wales coast line (Anglesey)
Located at the south end of the
station on the up side of the line, this
LNWR-type box opened in 1904,
and is now a Grade II listed building.
It controls entry into a siding (and
triangle), as well as the nearby road
crossing. *22.6.1993*

WALNUT TREE JUNCTION
Cardiff-Pontypridd line by Taffs Well station
The box is on the west side of the line and is a Taff Vale design of about 1910. It closed on 27 January 1997, and the view is looking north. *2.9.1994*

WHITLAND (W)   B:C4
Carmarthen-Fishguard Harbour line, junction of Pembroke Dock branch
The box is situated at the Carmarthen end of the station, on the down side. A BR (WR) design, it opened on 2 September 1972 when it replaced Whitland East and West boxes. The box and frame came from Danygraig. *29.6.1994*

YSTRAD MYNACH SOUTH (YM)
Rhymney Valley line
The box is south of the station on the west side of the line, and is photographed here from a passing train. It is a McKenzie & Holland/Rhymney design, and opened in about 1890. *27.7.1995*

There are a number of preserved signal boxes in
Wales, of which the following are two
examples.

BARMOUTH SOUTH   A:D5
Cambrian coast line
The box was on the south side of the road crossing by Barmouth station, seen here with two Crosville buses beyond. Of
Dutton (Cambrian) design, it officially closed in 1988. There is a plaque marking the site, which states that the box was
erected in 1883 and dismantled in 1999, following which it found a home with the Llangollen Railway at Glyndyfrdwy.
1985

LLANDRINDOD WELLS
B:G2
Central Wales line
This ex-LNWR box dating back to
1876 is now a museum and open to
the public. It closed in 1986 and in
1989 was moved a short distance
from Brooklands Road level crossing,
north of the station, to the down
platform. It is believed to be the most
southerly preserved LNWR signal
box in Wales. *9.6.1992*